Good Morning Sunday Cookery Book

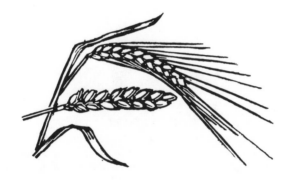

ROGER ROYLE

was born in Cardiff. He was educated at St Edmund's School,
Canterbury and later studied theology at King's College, London. In 1962 he
was ordained as a member of the Church of England in Portsmouth
Cathedral. During his full time ministry he has served in parishes in
Portsmouth, South London and the Thames Valley; St Helier and Guy's
Hospitals and Eton College where he was senior Chaplain.
Over the past ten years Roger Royle's ministry has changed. Although still
licensed to serve as a priest in the Diocese of Southwark, he earns his living
as a broadcaster and a writer. He still does a great deal of preaching,
speaking and fund-raising for charities but over the past few years he has
become known for his association with such programmes as Songs of Praise
and BBC Radio 2's Good Morning Sunday.

HILARY MAYO

has been producing Good Morning Sunday *since January 1988 and in 1989*
she organised the BBC Festival of Gospel Music for Radio 2. She read History
of Art and Design at Manchester Polytechnic where she acquired a passion
for Clarice Cliff pottery! Her first job was in her home town, at BBC Radio
Nottingham, where she ran the Helpline TXRX and met her
husband, Simon.

GOOD MORNING SUNDAY COOKERY BOOK

Compiled and edited by Hilary Mayo

Foreword by Roger Royle

❧ BBC BOOKS ❧

Published by BBC Books
A division of BBC Enterprises Limited
Woodlands, 80 Wood Lane
London W12 0TT

First published 1989
© Hilary Mayo and the Contributors 1990

© Foreword Roger Royle 1990

ISBN 0 563 20894 5

Typeset in Trump Mediaeval by
Goodfellow and Egan Photosetting Ltd, Cambridge
Printed and bound in Great Britain by Richard Clay Ltd, Bungay
Cover printed by Richard Clay Ltd, Norwich

❧ CONTENTS ❧

Dishes which can be prepared in advance are denoted by the symbol ◯.

❀ FOREWORD BY ROGER ROYLE ❀

I have to admit that presenting *Good Morning Sunday* plays havoc with my digestion. Before I leave for Broadcasting House I have one mug of tea – well possibly two. When I arrive at the studio, I am fed on a diet of coffee, generally black, and, if I am good, orange juice. But I have to wait until after 9 a.m. before I can really enjoy a plate of baked beans on toast in the BBC canteen and so give myself that fibre which is so essential for a balanced diet.

Actually, as many people know, maintaining a balanced diet is no easy achievement. And I have to say that I don't think the *Good Morning Sunday* Cookery Book is going to help you achieve it. Thanks to the interest of many listeners and a great number of guests that have appeared on the programme, we seem to have compiled a book of feasts. Fasts do get a look-in, but the emphasis is certainly on feasts. Every meal is a feast, no matter what the menu consists of, and I certainly hope that many of the recipes will be enjoyed by families and friends gathered together around a table. There is no better way to get to know people than at a meal. It is no wonder that Jesus instituted the Holy Communion at a meal, for it was at that meal He showed how well He really knew those who had been His companions for the previous three years. He also realised that it would be around similar tables that Christians, throughout history, would get to know one another and, more importantly, get to know Him. This is why He commanded that His followers should repeat that meal over and over again.

Sadly, many people, because of various pressures, have come to rely on instant food, eaten on the run. While others, who have all the time in the world to sit down and have a meal, eat alone. If this cookery book helps to bring people together round a meal table then it will have been worthwhile.

Others also will benefit from this book. We always need to be aware that although most of us in this country do not have to worry about where the next meal is coming from, there are millions of people of all ages in other parts of the world for whom food is very scarce and choice is non-existent. And so the royalties from this book will be given to Christian Aid and CAFOD (The Catholic Fund for Overseas Development) for their work overseas, and to The Arthritis and Rheumatism Council for Research for their demanding work in this country.

I should like to say thank you to all those who have contributed to this book, whether their recipe has been included or not; to Hilary Mayo and Jenny Pitt for compiling the book, and to Wendy Hobson for checking the recipes.

So all that remains to be said is, 'For what we are about to receive may the Lord make us truly thankful.'

✖ INTRODUCTION ✖

The idea for a *Good Morning Sunday* Cookery Book first came to me during a visit to Atlanta, Georgia, USA in 1988. I was there with Roger and the rest of the *Good Morning Sunday* team to make a special Easter edition of the programme to mark the twentieth anniversary of the death of the great civil rights leader, Dr Martin Luther King, Jr. It was a moving experience meeting his family and friends. We visited the house where he grew up, the office where he worked and the Ebenezer Baptist Church, where he had been co-pastor along with his father. Sitting there during a packed service we heard his youngest daughter, Bernice, preach from the pulpit where her father had stood many times and from where he had preached his first sermon aged a mere seventeen years old.

In the foyer of the church notices were laid out and booklets were for sale, including a cookery book that had been compiled by members of the congregation. The whole church family had been involved by contributing recipes and copies were being sold to raise money for church funds. I thought it would be a lovely souvenir of my visit so I bought a copy to bring home.

Good Morning Sunday is like a very large family and we therefore like to run projects that every member can be involved with. Last year listeners grew their own Bible gardens using *Good Morning Sunday* Bible seeds. With this book, many listeners and past guests have been involved by sending their favourite family recipes. Roger asked for unusual traditional dishes and the response has been incredible. I would like to thank everyone who took the trouble to write and those who have revealed their long-held family secrets with recipes that go back several generations. I am sorry if your recipe does not appear, but there was only space for a small percentage of all those sent to us – I only wish I could include them all!

The first four chapters represent the seasons and take us through the church festivals and feast days, starting with Advent, which marks the beginning of the Church Year. The origin, traditions and customs of each festival or feast day are explained, followed by all the recipes most appropriate for the occasion. If a particular date in the Church Year has been omitted this is because the book only covers events for which we received recipes.

At the end of each of the first four chapters is a section for Sunday lunches. This is specially for those of you who go to church *and* cook Sunday lunch . . . if you are one of those who has to balance this juggling act, how do you plan your morning? Do you put the roast in the oven before you go to church, then sneak out during the last hymn to ensure it does not overcook? Or do you wait until after church before you start to prepare the meal? – in which case you will not get lunch until mid-afternoon! This is a problem for many church-goers, particularly when you have friends coming for lunch, and especially for those who enjoy the increasingly popular practice of staying for coffee after the service. So apart from lots of new ideas for Sunday lunch, these chapters include dishes that can be prepared in advance and these are denoted by this symbol ○. Obviously there are many other recipes – such as cakes, Christmas puddings and ice-creams – which can or should be prepared in advance, but we have highlighted only those which may not be immediately obvious.

The fifth chapter is a selection of Jewish recipes and these contributions have been compiled separately for ease of access, as Jewish cooking is quite distinctive and relates to completely different festivals. Again, each of the festivals for which we received recipes have an explanation about origin, customs and traditions.

All the royalties from the book will be donated to charity, as Roger explains in his Foreword, and we will be having regular 'cookery spots' on *Good Morning Sunday* with Delia Smith and Rabbi Lionel Blue (Sundays, 7.30 a.m. – 9.00 a.m., Radio 2), so I hope you will be listening.

I have found writing and compiling this book quite fascinating and great fun. My sincere thanks goes to everyone who has assisted in some way, especially to Hyam Corney at *The Jewish Chronicle*, and to my Production Assistant, Jenny Pitt, who has spent endless hours typing!

I have said enough, so now may I wish you happy reading, happy cooking and happy eating!

(Hilary Mayo, producer, Good Morning Sunday)

1
Winter

✦ ADVENT ✦

Advent begins on the fourth Sunday before Christmas, the nearest to St Andrew's Day, and marks the beginning of the Church Year.

Advent is from the Latin word, 'adventus', meaning 'coming' or 'arrival', as it is the season of preparation for Christ's coming. Originally this was a period of fasting and prayer before the Nativity. Today it is more a time of joyful anticipation and preparation. Popular customs include advent calendars which originated in Germany, but came to us via the USA in the 1950s, and the advent wreath which can be seen in many churches throughout the country. The evergreen ring has four red candles and one is lit each Sunday until Christmas (when some add a white candle to the centre). This signifies the coming of Christ, the Light of the World.

Advent is heralded by *Stir-up Sunday*, which is the week before the start of this season and takes its name from the Collect for the twenty-fifth Sunday after Trinity, in the Book of Common Prayer,

'Stir up, we beseech thee, O Lord the wills of thy faithful people: that they, plenteously bringing forth the fruit of good works, may be of thee plenteously rewarded.'

Traditionally, this was the time when families would 'stir-up' their Christmas puddings and mincemeat – in order to give time for the mixture to mature for Christmas Day. The custom is that each member of the family should be invited to stir the mixture and make a wish, to bring good luck during the following year.

The origins of Christmas pudding can be traced back to the sixteenth century when it started life as a 'plum porridge' of beef broth, prunes, wine, breadcrumbs, mace and fruit juice. This rather sloppy mixture thickened during the seventeenth century and it was then they learned that if the mincemeat mixture was soaked in brandy and the meat was added only when ready to eat, it could be made well in advance of Christmas. Soon after this discovery, they started leaving out the meat altogether. By the end of the eighteenth century it was solid enough to be rolled into a ball and boiled in a cloth. Today it is usual to steam the Christmas pudding in a basin, an idea that was introduced by the Victorians. It is said that the dish was a great favourite of Prince Albert's.

An important part of today's preparation for the Christmas celebrations still involves cooking this traditional fare. Christmas pudding, mincemeat and Christmas cake all improve their flavour with keeping, so the beginning of Advent is a good time to make them. Under this heading are the traditional recipes and many unusual variations that you might like to try for a change.

❦ CHRISTMAS PUDDINGS ❧

The Legend of the Christmas Pudding

From Mr P. V. Dransfield, Paignton, Devon

Legend has it that a certain English king, who is conveniently anonymous, returned from hunting one Christmas Eve, gave his cook the fruit, nuts, flour, eggs and beer that his subjects had provided as gifts, and told him to make something tasty. The resourceful man mixed the lot, put it into a bag and boiled it for a time. So the first Christmas pudding was born.

When King George I, who reigned over England from 1714 to 1727, arrived here from Hanover, he was delighted with the cuisine in the country of his adoption, but particularly enchanted with the pudding that was made for him at Christmas. The original recipe has survived and it is now traditionally eaten on Christmas Day, after the roast turkey.

Traditional Christmas Plum Pudding

From Margaret Johnson, Elstree, Hertfordshire

This original family recipe has been handed down from generation to generation for at least 150 years, apparently from an ancestress who was cook in a large country rectory early in the nineteenth century.

Makes 3×3-pint (1.75-l) puddings

1 lb (450 g) shredded suet
1 lb (450 g) seedless raisins
1 lb (450 g) currants
1 lb (450 g) sultanas
8 oz (225 g) self-raising flour
8 oz (225 g) fresh white
  breadcrumbs
6 oz (175 g) chopped mixed peel
2 oz (50 g) citron or lime peel
  (optional)

1 lb (450 g) dark brown sugar
2 oz (50 g) almonds, chopped
3 teaspoons mixed spice (or to taste)
½ nutmeg, grated
1 carrot, grated
Grated rind and juice of 1 lemon
6 eggs
A little milk
1×14 fl oz (400 ml) bottle stout or
  old ale

Mix all the ingredients together thoroughly. The puddings should be mixed the day before cooking and left to stand overnight. The mixture should be a slightly soft, moist, dropping consistency. Fill 3×3-pint (1.75-l) basins to within about 1 in (2.5 cm) of the top. Tie buttered greaseproof paper firmly over the rims of the basins, and then tie over a further covering of white cotton or linen (old, clean, sheeting or tea towels are ideal for this).

Steam each basin in a saucepan of boiling water for approximately 6 hours, topping up the water as necessary. Alternatively cook in a pressure cooker for 2 hours. When cool, replace the covering cloths with clean, dry material and keep in a cool place until needed. The puddings will happily wait (and, indeed, improve) for a year until the following Christmas.

Re-heat on Christmas Day, either by steaming for approximately 2 hours, or by re-heating in a microwave oven according to the manufacturer's instructions.

Serve, flambé, with a sprig of holly on the top. Rum sauce and/or brandy butter are excellent accompaniments. A set of traditional silver charms, adroitly inserted at the last minute if you wish, can add to the general enjoyment; but warn guests to look out for these, especially the little ones.

Lincolnshire Christmas Pudding

From Mrs Annie Pocklington, Boston, Lincolnshire

This is a very old recipe. I am nearing eighty years old and this came to me by way of my mother-in-law's stepmother. My family have always insisted I keep it in the family but yours is a good cause. The original recipe makes enough mixture to fill five quart basins but I have whittled it down to make one fair sized pudding. The old saying which goes with this pudding is, 'carrots to darken, potatoes to lighten the texture'.

Makes 1 × 2½-pint (1.5-l) pudding

6 oz (175 g) currants
3 oz (75 g) seedless raisins
3 oz (75 g) sultanas
6 oz (175 g) sugar
3 oz (75 g) chopped mixed peel
6 oz (175 g) carrots, grated

6 oz (175 g) potatoes, grated
4 oz (100 g) breadcrumbs
4 oz (100 g) shredded suet
1 teaspoon ground nutmeg (or to taste)

Mix all the ingredients well and bind together with a little flour. Place in a pudding basin and cover with greased greaseproof paper, then with a cotton or muslin cloth. Tie securely with string. Place in a saucepan of water, bring to the boil and steam for 5 hours, topping up the water as necessary. Replace with clean covering and store in a cool place. When required, steam for 2 hours before serving.

Frozen Christmas Pudding

From Barbara Fawers, Woldingham, Surrey

A nice alternative to the usual suet pudding.

Makes 1 × 2-pint (1.2-l) pudding

3 egg yolks
4 oz (100 g) caster sugar
1 oz (25 g) flour
½ pint (300 ml) milk, warmed
A few drops of vanilla flavouring
1 oz (25 g) glacé cherries, chopped
1 oz (25 g) angelica, chopped
1 oz (25 g) walnuts, chopped
1 oz (25 g) crystallised pineapple, chopped

1 oz (25 g) almonds, flaked
1 oz (25 g) seedless raisins
1 oz (25 g) currants
1 oz (25 g) sultanas
1 oz (25 g) chopped mixed peel
1 fl oz (25 ml) Madeira
1 fl oz (25 ml) brandy
¼ pint (150 ml) double cream, whipped

Bring some water to the boil in the bottom of a double saucepan. Beat the egg yolks, sugar and flour in the top of the double saucepan, then add the warmed milk and vanilla. Stir until thick; this takes some time. Allow the custard to cool, stirring to prevent a skin forming. Mix together all the fruit ingredients, then pour the Madeira and brandy over the fruit. Steep for 1 hour. Whip the cream into the custard. Fold in the fruit, turn into a pudding basin, cover and freeze. Turn the pudding out a few minutes before it is required.

Nicholas Parsons'
Brandied Fruit Mince Ice-cream

I am not very fond of the traditional rich Christmas pudding – especially if you have eaten all that turkey and stuffing – so I prefer this recipe because it is exciting and spicy, but less heavy.

Makes 3½ pints (2 litres)

1½ oz (40 g) butter or margarine
6 oz (175 g) seedless raisins
4 oz (100 g) sultanas
2 oz (50 g) currants
2 oz (50 g) chopped mixed peel
½ teaspoon almond essence
Grated rind of 1 orange
Grated rind of 1 lemon
1 cooking apple, finely chopped

½ cup crushed pineapple
1 teaspoon mixed spice
4 tablespoons caster sugar
2 oz (50 g) walnuts, chopped
1 tablespoon orange juice
2 tablespoons brandy
1¾ pints (1 litre) soft scoop ice-cream

Melt the butter or margarine in a saucepan and add the raisins, sultanas, currants, mixed peel, almond essence, orange and lemon rinds, apple, pineapple, mixed spice, caster sugar, walnuts, orange juice and brandy. Cover and simmer gently for about 30 minutes. Allow to cool. Spoon the ice-cream into a bowl and whip. Fold in the fruit mince mixture and then pour into freezing trays. Return to the freezer and freeze until set.

Traditional Mincemeat

From Mrs E. M. Sparrow, Llandudno, Gwynedd

This recipe has been passed down in our family for about 100 years.

Makes about 4 lb (1.75 kg) mincemeat

1 lb (450 g) cooking apples, peeled
and cored
8 oz (225 g) seedless raisins
8 oz (225 g) currants
8 oz (225 g) sultanas
2 oz (50 g) chopped mixed peel
1 lb (450 g) sugar

4 oz (100 g) shredded suet
Juice of ½ lemon
Juice of ½ orange
¼ teaspoon salt
½ teaspoon nutmeg (or to taste)
1 wine glass rum or brandy

Mince the apples and dried fruit. Mix all the ingredients together. Stir well and allow to stand overnight. Put into clean, air-tight jars and store in a cool place until required.

Rustie Lee's Caribbean Christmas Cake

Each year when I prepare my cake ready for Christmas, my memory always takes me back to the hilarious time that I had in the TV AM Kitchen mixing all the ingredients with Jimmy Tarbuck, helped along by the Jamaican rum – havoc ensued.

Makes 1 × 12-in (30-cm) cake

1 lb (450 g) sultanas
2 lb (1 kg) mixed fruit
8 oz (225 g) seedless raisins
8 oz (225 g) currants
4 oz (100 g) glacé cherries, chopped
1 bottle ruby wine
1 lb (450 g) butter
1 lb (450 g) soft brown sugar
10 eggs, beaten

1 tablespoon caramel colouring or
treacle (to taste)
1 lb (450 g) plain flour
4 oz (100 g) ground almonds
1 dessertspoon cinnamon
1 dessertspoon nutmeg
1 dessertspoon vanilla essence
1 dessertspoon rum flavouring
1 bottle rum

Pre-heat the oven to 325°F (160°C), gas mark 3.

Steam all the fruit together in the ruby wine for about 15 minutes. Allow to cool. Cream the butter and sugar together until light and fluffy then gradually add the eggs and caramel colouring. Mix the flour and the ground almonds, then add the cinnamon and nutmeg. Add the dry ingredients to the creamed butter and fold in. Mix all the fruit into the mixture, adding the vanilla essence and rum flavouring. Place into a well-lined, greased tin and bake in the oven for 3 hours. Allow the cake to cool, and then pour over the bottle of rum, allowing it to soak in. To keep the cake moist, wrap in foil until ready to decorate.

Christmas Vegetable Mincemeat

From Mrs B. Griffiths, Colchester, Essex

Because I am on a strict diet 'normal' sweet mincemeat is 'out'. This recipe means I can enjoy mince tarts like everyone else and not be left out at Christmas. It tastes incredibly like 'the real thing'.

Makes about 8 oz (225 g) mincemeat

3 oz (75 g) carrot, grated
2 oz (50 g) parsnip, chopped
A few almonds, flaked
1 tablespoon preserved ginger,
  chopped
1 tablespoon dark brown sugar
¼ teaspoon grated nutmeg
¼ teaspoon mace
¼ teaspoon cinnamon
1 tablespoon desiccated coconut
A little whisky or rum (optional)

For the sweet sauce
4 oz (100 g) butter or margarine
2 oz (50 g) caster sugar
2 oz (50 g) icing sugar
2 oz (50 g) ground almonds
2–3 tablespoons whisky or brandy

Place the carrot and parsnip in saucepan with a little water. Bring to the boil and cook until soft. Then add all the other ingredients except the whisky or rum, and boil for about 15 to 20 minutes. A little whisky or rum can be added at this stage, if liked. If there is too much liquid, add a tablespoon of ground almonds and cook for a few more minutes.

To make a sweet sauce to serve with the mince tarts, beat together the butter or margarine, caster sugar, icing sugar, ground almonds and whisky or brandy. Store in the refrigerator for 1 hour before serving.

Delia Smith's Christmas Mincemeat Cake

My husband, Michael, assures me that this is delicious!

Makes 1 × 8-in (20-cm) cake

1 lb (450 g) mincemeat
8 oz (225 g) wholewheat flour
3 teaspoons baking powder
5 oz (150 g) dark brown sugar
5 oz (150 g) soft margarine
6 oz (175 g) mixed dried fruit
2 oz (50 g) walnuts, chopped

Grated zest of 1 small orange
Grated zest of 1 small lemon
3 eggs
2 oz (50 g) whole blanched almonds
  (omit if you are going to ice the
  cake)

Pre-heat the oven to 325°F (160°C), gas mark 3.

First of all, prepare an 8-in (20-cm) cake tin by lining the base and sides with greaseproof paper. Place all the ingredients (except the almonds) in a large mixing bowl – there is no need to beat the eggs, just break them in. It's a good idea to sift the flour to give it an airing, tipping in the bits of bran left in the sieve afterwards.

Now, if you have an electric hand-whisk, just switch on and beat everything together thoroughly. If not, a wooden spoon will do, but will take a bit longer. Next, spoon the mixture evenly into the tin, level off the surface, and arrange the almonds in circles over the top.

Bake for about 1 hour 20 minutes, or until the centre springs back when lightly touched. Let it cool in the tin for 30 minutes then finish cooling on a wire rack. Store in an air-tight container.

White Christmas Cake

From Mrs Elizabeth Merry, Wingham, Canterbury

This is just as good even if there is no snow! It is also a lovely cake for Christmas because of the seasonal colours of the red, green, yellow and brown fruits.

Makes 1 × 8-in (20-cm) cake

4 oz (100 g) glacé cherries
4 oz (100 g) glacé pineapple
4 oz (100 g) crystallised ginger
1 oz (25 g) angelica
4 oz (100 g) sultanas
4 oz (100 g) chopped mixed peel
3 tablespoons brandy

12 oz (350 g) plain flour
9 oz (250 g) butter
9 oz (250 g) caster sugar
4 large eggs, beaten
4 oz (100 g) walnuts, coarsely
  chopped

Pre-heat the oven to 300°F (150°C), gas mark 2.

Wash the syrup coating from the cherries, pineapple, ginger and angelica with warm water, then pat dry on kitchen paper. Cut the cherries in half and coarsely chop the pineapple, ginger and angelica. Put the fruits in a basin with the sultanas, mixed peel and the brandy. Leave to soak overnight. Sift the flour on to a square of greaseproof paper and set aside. Cream the butter and sugar until light and fluffy. Mix the eggs and gradually beat into the creamed mixture a little at a time, adding some of the sifted flour with the last few additions of egg. Using a metal spoon, gradually fold in the remaining flour, then the soaked fruits with any liquid, and finally the walnuts. Spoon the mixture into a greased and lined 8-in (20-cm) round deep cake tin. Spread the mixture evenly and hollow out the centre. Bake below the centre in a cool oven for 2½ to 3 hours. Leave in the tin until quite cold. The cake can be eaten as it is, or decorated with a thin skin of marzipan and royal icing.

Festival Ring Cake

From Mrs Christine McLaren, Hedon, Hull, North Humberside

Makes 1×8-in (20-cm) cake

4 oz (100 g) soft margarine
5 oz (150 g) self-raising flour
½ teaspoon baking powder
4 oz (100 g) caster sugar
2 eggs
3 tablespoons milk

For the icing
6 oz (175 g) granulated sugar
1 egg white
3 tablespoons cold water
½ teaspoon vanilla essence

Pre-heat the oven to 375°F (190°C), gas mark 5.

Lightly grease an 8-in (20-cm) ring cake tin. Put all the ingredients into a mixing bowl and beat well with a wooden spoon until smooth. Spoon the mixture into the tin. Bake in a moderately hot oven for 30 to 35 minutes. Cool on a wire rack.

To make the icing, place all the icing ingredients in a bowl over boiling water. Whisk until smooth and thick. Spread over the cake to give a rough finish. Leave to set. Place the cake on silver board if desired.

For Advent   Add a few drops of green colouring to the icing. Decorate with angelica and violets. Place a tall purple candle in the centre.

For Christmas   Leave the icing white. Decorate with silver balls and holly leaves. Place a tall red candle in the centre.

For Easter   Add a few drops of yellow colouring to the icing. Decorate with yellow and white sugar flowers. Place a tall white candle in the centre, or a vase or fish-paste jar filled with tiny spring flowers.

Celebration Cake

From Mrs Chris Whitaker, Boston Spa, Wetherby, West Yorkshire

This recipe has been passed down through my mother's family for several generations – well over 100 years. I always make it for Christmas, anniversaries, christenings – in short anything we want to celebrate.

Makes 1×8×8×3-in (20×20×7.5-cm) cake

4 oz (100 g) black treacle, warmed
12 oz (350 g) butter
12 oz (350 g) soft brown sugar
6 large eggs
4 oz (100 g) ground almonds
7 fl oz (200 ml) tepid milk
1 lb (450 g) currants
1 lb (450 g) seedless raisins
1 lb (450 g) sultanas
1 teaspoon mixed spice
1 lb (450 g) plain flour
2½–3 fl oz (65–85 ml) brandy, to
  pour on the bottom of the cake
  when it comes out of the oven

For the almond icing
6 oz (175 g) icing sugar
10 oz (275 g) caster sugar
1 lb (450 g) ground almonds
1 large egg
1 egg yolk
Juice of ½ lemon
1 tablespoon brandy
½ teaspoon vanilla essence
2 drops almond essence

Pre-heat the oven to 250°F (120°C), gas mark ½.
  Weigh out the treacle and put it in a warm place. Cream the butter and sugar until light and fluffy. Add the eggs one at a time, beating after each addition. Add the rest of the ingredients, except the brandy, in the order in which they are listed, mixing each one in before adding the next. Lastly fold in the flour. Grease a double-bottomed 8×8×3-in (20×20×7.5-cm) cake tin with butter or margarine (if your tin has only a single thickness on the bottom, cook the mixture standing the tin on a baking tray). Line the bottom and sides with a double layer of greaseproof paper. The paper round the sides should stand up at least 1 in (2.5 cm) above the edge of the tin. Fill with the mixture and bake in the oven, one shelf below the middle, for 6½ hours. When cooked, remove from the oven and immediately turn out on to a wire cake rack, the bottom of the cake uppermost. Carefully peel off the paper. As soon as you have done this, trickle the brandy all over the bottom of the cake. Leave to cool completely. When cold wrap in foil, put in an air-tight tin and store for 2 to 3 months.
  To make the almond icing, sieve the icing sugar and caster sugar together and mix in the ground almonds. Beat the egg and yolk and add lemon juice, brandy, vanilla and almond essence. Pour on to the almond and sugar mixture and mix well. Roll out and use to cover the cake.

Tipsy-Cake

From Mrs P. J. Finnie, North Cray, Sidcup, Kent

This is a recipe that I make mostly at Christmas, as it makes a change from the traditional Christmas cake.

Makes 1×8-in (20-cm) cake

8 oz (225 g) dried apricots, chopped
4 oz (100 g) seedless raisins
4 fl oz (120 ml) brandy
4 fl oz (120 ml) unsweetened orange
  juice
6 oz (175 g) self-raising flour

2 teaspoons baking powder
6 oz (175 g) margarine
4 tablespoons honey
4 large eggs, separated
Icing sugar

Pre-heat the oven to 350°F (180°C), gas mark 4.
Put the apricots and raisins in a saucepan. Pour in the brandy and orange juice. Bring to the boil, stir well, then remove from the heat and leave to cool for 1 hour. Sift the flour and baking powder. Cream the margarine and honey, then beat in the egg yolks one at a time. Stir in 1 tablespoon of flour and the apricot mixture, then add the remaining flour. Whisk the egg whites until stiff, then fold them into the mixture a little at a time. Place the mixture in a greased and lined 8-in (20-cm) cake tin and bake in the oven on the lower centre shelf for 60 to 70 minutes. When cooked, leave in the tin for 10 minutes before turning out and allowing to cool completely. Sprinkle with icing sugar before serving.

Yuletide-after-Carolling Punch

From Mrs Gwen Aird, Willowbank, Wick, Caithness

This is an old Canadian recipe; a flask of vodka can be added, if desired.

Makes about 8 pints (4.5 l)

2 pints (1.2 l) unsweetened
  pineapple juice
6 oz (175 g) white sugar
1 large can pink lemonade (or
  lemonade with grape juice added)

16 fl oz (475 ml) water
3 pints (1.75 l) ginger ale
2 pints (1.2 l) strawberry ice-cream

Stir the pineapple juice, sugar, lemonade, water and ginger ale until the sugar has dissolved. Spoon the ice-cream on top of the punch. Place in the refrigerator for 1 hour before serving.

❀ CHRISTMAS ❀

'Today in the town of David a Saviour has been born to you; he is Christ the Lord . . . you will find a baby wrapped in cloths and lying in a manger.' (Luke 2 : 11 & 12)

Christmas Day in the Western Church is always 25 December and it is the date chosen to celebrate the birth of Jesus Christ. For many Christians, this festival begins with Midnight Mass on Christmas Eve. The church, lit by candle light, is decked with holly and ivy, and the congregation sing traditional Christmas carols like 'Away In a Manger' and 'O Come All Ye Faithful'. The date of Christmas was decided upon in the fourth century to coincide with the ancient pagan celebrations of the Winter Solstice and it is thought this was done in order to attract the interest of the many non-Christians. It is also exactly nine months after the date of the Annunciation or Conception on 25 March.

There are probably more customs associated with this festival than any other in the Church Year. Many, it seems, began as features of the pagan festivals, but Christians adopted the ideas, and gave them new religious significance. For example, the giving of gifts symbolises the offerings made to the Christ child by the Wise Men, and the spices in the mincemeat that we traditionally eat at Christmas were originally said to represent those brought by the Three Kings. However, it was during the Victorian era that Christmas as we know it today really took shape. The idea of sending special greeting cards was first introduced and in 1840 Prince Albert brought the first Christmas tree from his native Germany.

Father Christmas, or Santa Claus, came to us in the 1870s from the USA where Dutch settlers took with them the legend of St Nicholas, Bishop of Myra. The story goes that he would visit all good children on Christmas Eve, leaving them toys and sweets. Over the years he has lost his Bishop's robes for the now familiar red and white costume.

Other Christmas customs include the burning of the yule log. Traditionally lit on Christmas Eve and kept burning for the Twelve Days of Christmas, the remains were kept to kindle the next year's yule fire. A crib or nativity scene can be found in many homes and churches, and this idea comes to us from St Francis of Assisi who made the first crib in the thirteenth century.

Christmas has always been a time of celebration and feasting. The favourite Christmas dinner at the manor house in medieval times would have been a boar's head or some sort of fowl such as a swan or a peacock. By the Tudor period, these had lost favour and roast beef was the order of the day. Turkey was first brought to Britain in the mid-sixteenth century and by the 1590s it had become very popular. However, it is only relatively recently that it has been the custom to eat roast turkey for Christmas dinner. Prior to that, goose, chicken and roast beef were the favourites.

Today, the custom is to eat turkey with potatoes, Brussels sprouts, stuffings, bread and cranberry sauces, followed by Christmas pudding and brandy butter or white sauce.

Mince pies have been popular since the reign of Elizabeth I. Originally they were savoury, made with fat mutton and eaten before the meal. It is also said that the pastry cases used to represent Christ's manger, much to the distaste of the Puritans who thought them 'idolatrous'!

In the north of England, during the eighteenth century, spicy fruit and yeast cakes, called Yule Cake or Doos, were eaten hot with Wensleydale cheese and mulled wine. But probably the oldest dish still known to us is Frumerty, traditionally one of the main features of the Christmas Eve supper. The wealthy would use it as an accompaniment to the meat, such as venison, while the poor ate it on its own as a sweet dish flavoured with spices and currants. In parts of Yorkshire it was eaten with gingerbread.

Hot Christmas Punch

From Mrs P. Spinks, Torquay

Serves 6

1 bottle red wine	1 good slice lemon, stuck with 12 to
1 cinnamon stick, broken into	15 cloves
pieces	

Heat the ingredients in a pan until hot, but do not boil. Transfer when hot into a well warmed punch bowl, and ladle generously into glasses.

Walnut and Cheese Savouries

From Mrs Pat Tonks, Wychbold, near Droitwich, Worcestershire

These tasty cheese pastries make a delicious appetiser to serve with sherry. I usually make a batch at Christmas as they will keep in an air-tight container for three weeks and prove very useful to have handy for unexpected callers who drop in – sometimes with presents!

Makes about 16 savouries

3 oz (75 g) butter or margarine
4 oz (100 g) plain flour (plus extra
 for rolling out)
Salt

3 oz (75 g) cheese, finely grated
1 egg, lightly beaten
1 oz (25 g) walnuts, finely chopped

Pre-heat the oven to 350°F (180°C), gas mark 4.
Lightly grease a baking tray. Rub the butter or margarine into the flour and add a pinch of salt. Add the cheese and mix in with the fingertips. (Make sure your hands are cool because of the quantity of fat in the mixture. Use your fingertips only and stop if the mixture starts to stick to your fingers.) Add the beaten egg and mix to a firm dough (you may not need all the egg). Roll the mixture into a rectangle ¼-in (5-mm) thick, and keep it moving. Trim the edges. Cut into 2×3-in (7.5-cm) wide strips and sprinkle with salt. Brush with egg and sprinkle with salt again, if desired. Sprinkle with the walnuts and cut into triangles. Bake in the oven for 15 to 20 minutes, until the savouries are golden brown and sizzling.
The savouries can be piped with cream cheese when cool, if liked.

Sir Peter Imbert's
New Romney Rabbit Pie

This used to be cooked by my mother at Christmas time. Nowadays, in deference to the vegetarians in my family, as well as the traditional fare, nut roast features on the table at Christmas too!

Serves 4 to 6

1 rabbit, jointed
1 large onion, sliced
1 teaspoon mixed herbs

12 oz (350 g) unsmoked streaky
 bacon, cut into pieces
Salt and pepper
12 oz (350 g) short pastry

Pre-heat the oven to 400°F (200°C), gas mark 6.

Place the rabbit joints into a saucepan with the sliced onion, cover with water and bring to the boil. Simmer for 5 to 10 minutes. Put into a 3-pint (1.75-l) casserole or pie dish, with ¼ pint (150 ml) of the fluid from the saucepan. Add the herbs, bacon and seasoning and cooked onion. Cover with the pastry, placing a pie funnel under the pastry to keep the shape. Bake in the oven for 30 to 40 minutes till the top is golden brown.

This is delicious served cold with a green salad and sliced beetroot.

Christmas Nut Roast

From Mrs Barbara Boiling, Chaddesden, Derby

I'm sure a great number of Christians like me find the cruel and inhumane methods of rearing animals and birds for food, together with their eventual slaughter, totally abhorrent and irreconcilable with the birth of the Prince of Peace. I therefore suggest this delicious alternative dish to the traditional one of turkey.

Serves 4

4 oz (100 g) wholemeal breadcrumbs
2 oz (50 g) cashews, ground or chopped
2 oz (50 g) hazelnuts, ground or chopped
2 oz (50 g) sunflower seeds, ground or chopped
1 medium apple, grated
1 medium carrot, grated
½ teaspoon fresh chopped or dried thyme
½ teaspoon fresh chopped or dried rosemary

Sea salt and freshly ground black pepper
1 large onion, finely chopped
1 clove garlic, crushed
4 oz (100 g) mushrooms, finely sliced
½ red pepper, chopped (optional)
½ green pepper, chopped (optional)
1 teaspoon Barmene or Tartex (or Marmite), dissolved in about ½ cup hot water
½ pint (300 ml) tomato juice

Pre-heat the oven to 400°F (200°C), gas mark 6.

Combine the breadcrumbs, nuts, seeds, grated apple and carrot, herbs and seasoning to taste, in a large mixing bowl. Lightly sauté the onion, garlic, mushrooms and peppers in a little oil, and add to the above mixture. Add the diluted Barmene and enough tomato juice to bind and form a fairly moist dropping consistency. Place in a greased ovenproof dish or a 2-lb (1-kg) loaf tin. Bake in the oven for 45 to 60 minutes, or until golden brown on top. Decorate with fresh herbs and slices of tomato, if desired.

Goose Pudding

From Mrs Anne Errington, Billingham, Cleveland

This is a Christmas recipe that was handed down to my grandma when Billingham was a village and her family lived on one of the many farms. It is still a great favourite with our family. The purpose of the 'pudding' was the same as Yorkshire pudding – to take the edge off the appetite, in this case before the Christmas goose.

Serves 4

8 oz (225 g) breadcrusts
3 oz (75 g) shredded suet, chopped
2 tablespoons oatmeal (porridge
oats are best)
Salt and pepper
½ tablespoon sage

2 large onions, boiled and chopped
¼ tablespoon marjoram
1 egg
¼ pint (150 ml) milk
½ oz (15 g) dripping

Pre-heat the oven to 425°F (220°C), gas mark 7.

Soak the bread in cold water until soft. Drain all the water away and squeeze the bread as dry as possible, then beat it with a fork. Add all the other dry ingredients and mix with the egg and milk. Heat the dripping in a baking tin. Spread the mixture in the tin and bake in a hot oven for about 45 minutes. Let it stand for a few minutes, then cut it into squares and serve with gravy.

It is as good or even better after re-heating – always supposing there's any left!

Anne Shelton's
Seasoned Yorkshire Pudding

This recipe, which has been in my family for quite a time, was given to my grandmother by a friend in Bradford. It is ideal served with the Christmas turkey or roast pork.

Serves 4 to 6

4 oz (100 g) plain flour
1 teaspoon salt
2 eggs
1 pint (600 ml) milk
1 medium onion, finely chopped

2 oz (50 g) shredded suet
1 very thick slice white bread,
grated into crumbs
1 level dessertspoon chopped sage
1 level dessertspoon chopped thyme

Pre-heat the oven to 350°F (180°C), gas mark 4.
Mix together the flour and salt, then gradually beat in the eggs. Once
smooth, add the milk to make Yorkshire pudding batter. Place the onion,
shredded suet, breadcrumbs, sage and thyme in a clean bowl and mix. Stir
this into the batter. Pour the batter into a hot greased 8×12-in (20×30-cm)
baking tin and cook in a moderate oven for 1½ hours. Increase the heat, if
you can, for the last ½ an hour to make it crisp.

Apricot Stuffing

From Mrs E. M. Bird, Burton Joyce, Nottingham

This is my family's favourite stuffing. It is good with pork and turkey, but
they like it with any meat. Always a must on Christmas Day!

Makes about 1¼ lb (500 g)

6 oz (175 g) breadcrumbs
*4 oz (100 g) dried apricots, finely
 chopped*
*2 oz (50 g) salted peanuts, finely
 chopped*
1 tablespoon chopped parsley

2 oz (50 g) butter
6 oz (175 g) onion, finely chopped
Grated rind and juice of 1 orange
¾ teaspoon curry powder
Salt and pepper
1 egg, beaten

Place the breadcrumbs, apricots, peanuts and parsley in a bowl. Melt the
butter in a small saucepan, add the onion and orange rind, cover and cook
gently until soft. Remove from the pan and add to the breadcrumb mixture.
Gently cook the curry powder in the pan for 1 minute, add 3 tablespoons of
orange juice and bubble gently for 30 seconds. Add to the breadcrumb
mixture. Season well and bind with beaten egg.

Chestnut and Onion Stuffing

From Mrs Margaret Yallop, Peterborough, Cambridgeshire

Use this recipe to stuff the neck of the turkey or chicken only. This stuffing is one of my favourites that I make for Christmas.

Makes about 1½ lb (750 g)

8 oz (225 g) chestnuts
2 oz (50 g) Brazil nuts, shelled
5 oz (150 g) onions
3 oz (75 g) margarine

3 oz (75 g) brown breadcrumbs
2 teaspoons fresh parsley
Juice of 1 lemon
Salt and pepper

Place the chestnuts in a saucepan of water and bring to the boil. Drain and allow to cool and then peel. Cook the shelled Brazil nuts in boiling water for 3 minutes, and then chop the chestnuts and Brazil nuts very finely. Fry the onions in the margarine. Add the breadcrumbs, nuts, parsley and lemon juice. Season to taste.

Luxury Mince Pies

From Mrs M. E. Daly, St Columb, Cornwall

Makes 12 mince pies

4 oz (100 g) butter
8 oz (225 g) plain flour
1 teaspoon caster sugar
Grated rind and juice of 1 orange

For the filling
8 oz (225 g) mincemeat
1–2 tablespoons rum or sherry

Pre-heat the oven to 400°F (200°C), gas mark 6.
Rub the butter into the flour until the mixture resembles fine breadcrumbs. Stir in the sugar and orange rind. Add sufficient orange juice to make a soft, but not sticky, dough. Roll out on a lightly floured surface and cut into 12 large and 12 small rounds. Line 12 lightly greased patty tins with the large rounds. Combine the mincemeat with the rum or sherry, and divide the filling between the cases. Dampen the edges with water. Press the lids in place and prick the tops with a fork. Bake in the centre of the oven for 20 minutes.

Chocolate Yule Log

From Mrs Janet M. Ashenden, Linton, Burton-on-Trent, Staffordshire

Makes 1×9-in (23-cm) log

3 eggs
4 oz (100 g) caster sugar
4 oz (100 g) plain flour
2 oz (50 g) plain chocolate, grated
1 tablespoon hot water

For the filling and icing
6 oz (175 g) butter
12 oz (350 g) icing sugar, sifted
1–2 tablespoons warm water
2 tablespoons cocoa dissolved in 1 tablespoon hot water
Holly, robin and icing sugar to decorate

Pre-heat the oven to 425°F (220°C), gas mark 7.

Line a 13×9-in (33×23-cm) swiss roll tin with greaseproof paper. Put the eggs and sugar in a large bowl, stand it over a pan of hot water, and whisk until light and creamy (the mixture should be stiff enough to retain the impression of the whisk for a few seconds). Remove the pan from the heat and whisk until cool. Sift half the flour over the mixture and fold in very lightly using a metal spoon. Add the grated chocolate, and the rest of the flour, and fold in lightly. Gently stir in the hot water. Pour the mixture into the prepared tin, tilting the tin so that it spreads evenly. Bake in the oven for 7 to 9 minutes, until well risen and spongy.

Meanwhile, have ready a sheet of greaseproof paper, liberally sprinkled with caster sugar. Turn the cake quickly out on to the paper, and trim off the crusty edges with a sharp knife. Cover the sponge with another sheet of greaseproof paper and roll it up loosely.

To make the buttercream, cream the butter until soft and gradually beat in the icing sugar. Beat in the water, and the cocoa. When the cake is cold, unroll it, remove the paper and spread half of the buttercream over the swiss roll, then roll it up again. Use the rest of the buttercream to cover the outside of the roll, then, using a fork, make lines down the log to make it look like bark. Decorate with holly and a plastic robin. Sieve a little icing sugar over the top to look like snow.

Christmas Shortbread ○

From Mrs Linda M. Ashworth, Kenilworth, Warwickshire

This is a recipe I only use at Christmas. It has become one of the traditions of Christmas in our house. I originally had the recipe from a 'Christmas Cookery' course I attended at Kirkley Hall, near Morpeth, Northumberland, during the first years of our marriage. The recipe always reminds me of our ten happy years in the north-east.

Makes about 12 fingers

3 oz (75 g) butter
3 oz (75 g) margarine
9 oz (250 g) plain flour
3 oz (75 g) sugar
For the topping
½ oz (15 g) almonds, chopped

½ oz (15 g) walnuts, chopped
1 oz (25 g) seedless raisins, chopped
1 oz (25 g) glacé cherries, chopped
Grated rind of 1 orange or 1 lemon
Caster sugar for sprinkling

Pre-heat the oven to 350°F (180°C), gas mark 4.
Rub the fat into the flour and sugar. Press the ingredients together firmly to form a paste. Knead until perfectly smooth, leaving no flour on the board. Press the paste into a swiss roll tin, making the surface flat with a palette knife. Sprinkle the surface with the topping ingredients and press them into the paste by rolling gently with the sides of a jam jar. Mark into fingers. Bake in the centre of the oven for 30 minutes. Sprinkle with caster sugar immediately the shortbread comes out of the oven. Re-cut between the sections and leave until cold. Store in an air-tight tin.

Lincolnshire Christmas Loaf ○

From Mrs G. S. Moynihan, Alton, Hampshire

Makes 1 × 1-lb (450-g) loaf

2 oz (50 g) lard
2 oz (50 g) butter or margarine
8 oz (225 g) plain flour
4 oz (100 g) sugar
1 tablespoon chopped mixed peel

8 oz (225 g) currants
½ teaspoon baking powder
A pinch of salt and nutmeg
¼ teaspoon bicarbonate of soda
* mixed in ¼ pint (150 ml) milk*

Pre-heat the oven to 275°F (140°C), gas mark 1.
Rub the fat into the flour. Add the other ingredients and mix with the milk to a fairly stiff mixture. Line a 1-lb (450-g) loaf tin with greased paper and fill with the mixture. Bake in the oven for 1½ hours, or until firm when tested. Cool and keep until required. Serve sliced and buttered.

Yule Doos

From Marjorie Turnbull, Billericay, Essex

Our family is the only one I have come across who have heard of these. But my grandmother made them for her family and I understand her mother made them before her. My aunt, who was the eldest in the family, was born in 1904, so this takes the tradition back well into the nineteenth century.

These delicious sweet buns are to be eaten on Christmas morning.

Makes 6 buns

1 lb (450 g) plain flour
2 oz (50 g) sugar
2 oz (50 g) chopped mixed peel
  (optional)
¼ teaspoon cassia and mace (or
  ½ teaspoon mixed spice)
1 oz (25 g) yeast

8 fl oz (250 ml) warm water
2 oz (50 g) currants
2 oz (50 g) sultanas
1 oz (25 g) margarine
1 oz (25 g) lard
1 egg

Pre-heat the oven to 400°F (200°C), gas mark 6.

Warm a mixing bowl, and put in the flour, sugar, peel, cassia and mace (or mixed spice). Mix well, then make well in centre. Sprinkle the yeast into the hole, and add a teaspoonful sugar and 4 fl oz (120 ml) of warm water. Put the bowl into warm place until the yeast bubbles, then beat well with wooden spoon. Soak the currants and sultanas in hot water. Melt, but do not boil, the margarine and lard in a saucepan. Beat the egg well with the remaining warm water, then add this to the yeast. Add the melted fat and gradually add the drained fruit. Mix to a light dough, and add more warm water if necessary, kneading in the bowl.

Cover the dough with a piece of greaseproof paper and a clean tea towel and put to rise in a warm place until the dough has doubled in size. Turn out on to a floured board and shape into 6 pieces. Knead them lightly and shape into ovals. Make cuts as shown on the diagram, fold the arms into the middle, and place currants for eyes, noses and buttons. Place on a baking tray in a warm place until they double in size again. Bake in the oven for 15 to 20 minutes. Cool on a wire tray, then brush with a little melted butter while they are still hot.

For boys   For girls

Christmas Jam

From Mrs Elizabeth Bollé, Kingsbury, London

Makes about 4 lb (1.75 kg)

2 lb (1 kg) cooking apples
1 pint (600 ml) water
1 lb (450 g) sultanas
2 oz (50 g) shredded lemon and
  orange peel
Juice and rind of 1 grapefruit or
  large orange

¼ teaspoon nutmeg
1 teaspoon ground ginger
1½ lb (750 g) sugar
1 teaspoon almond essence

Peel and core the apples, and put into a saucepan with the water, sultanas, peel, juice and rind of the grapefruit or orange, nutmeg and ginger. Boil these together gently until the apples and sultanas are tender. Add the sugar, and stir until dissolved. Boil for about 20 minutes until it sets. Stir in the almond essence, pour the jam into clean warm jars and seal. Delicious!

Frumerty

From Miss R. Spinks

Fifty years ago, in north-east England (especially in County Durham and the Yorkshire Dales) a dish of Frumerty was as much a part of Christmas Eve as hanging up stockings is today!

Serves 4 to 6

1 pint (600 ml) wheat
1 pint (600 ml) milk
1 pint (600 ml) water
2 tablespoons sugar (or to taste)

1 teaspoon cinnamon (optional)
1 teaspoon nutmeg (optional)
1 tablespoon honey (optional)
1 tablespoon currants (optional)

Pre-heat the oven to 300°F (150°C), gas mark 2.
  Soak the wheat in the milk and water. Place in a casserole dish, and sweeten with sugar. Cook for 3 hours in a cool oven until the mixture is thick and resembles jelly. You can flavour it with the cinnamon, nutmeg, honey and currants, if you wish. Serve hot with cream.
  To eat the Frumerty, the eldest two present eat from the dish together first, then the next two in age, and so on down to the youngest.

※ ST STEPHEN'S DAY (26 DECEMBER) ※

St Stephen's Day is more commonly known as 'Boxing Day', named after the custom of giving servants and employees a small gift of money or 'Christmas box' as a thank you for their work throughout the year. Today this custom benefits the milkman, postman and dustman. Boxing Day was also traditionally the time for hunting small animals, such as the squirrel and the wren.

St Stephen was the first male Christian martyr, one of seven deacons appointed by the Apostles to attend to the needs of the first Christian community in Jerusalem. *'A man full of faith and of the Holy Ghost'* (Acts 6 : 5), he was falsely accused of blasphemy and brought before the Council of the Jews (the Sanhedrin) whereupon he made a lengthy speech, concluding that Jesus, whom they had crucified, was the Messiah. With that they took him from the city and stoned him to death. Today St Stephen is remembered in the words of the popular Christmas carol, 'Good King Wenceslas looked out on the Feast of Stephen . . .'

As far as food is concerned, Boxing Day is a time for using up left-overs, so here are some ideas to liven up cold turkey and left-over Christmas pudding.

Devilled Turkey Legs

From Mrs H. Wright, Droitwich, Worcestershire

I am now aged eighty, but when I was a child at home, we only had turkey at Christmas. The legs were always kept to be used in this recipe for Boxing Day, and the chutney was always home-made marrow chutney.

Serves 4

4 cooked turkey legs	*4 tablespoons chutney*
2 tablespoons freshly mixed	*Flour*
mustard	*A little dripping*

Remove the skin from the turkey legs. Spread quite thickly with mustard and then with chutney. Dip the legs in the flour and fry in the dripping until they are hot inside and crisp on the outside. Remove the legs to a warm plate, pour off any excess fat from the pan and make a thick gravy in the pan incorporating any chutney pieces which may have fallen off.

Serve these tasty turkey legs with mashed potato and any other vegetable – a great way to use up left-overs.

Fred's Farewell

From Miss D. B. Turner, Shoeburyness, Essex

As a family, our Christmas turkey has always been nicknamed 'Fred', hence the name of the following recipe, using up the remains. Another excellent dish for left-overs.

Serves 4

1 lb (450 g) cooked turkey or chicken
4 oz (100 g) cooked peas
4 oz (100 g) cooked carrots, sliced
4 oz (100 g) Cheddar cheese, grated
1 × 14½-oz (415-g) tin sliced peaches, drained

1 × 11-oz (300-g) tin condensed mushroom soup
1 small packet potato crisps (plain or smoky bacon)

Pre-heat the oven to 400°F (200°C), gas mark 6.
   Grease a 2-pint (1.2-l) pie dish. Cut the turkey or chicken into bite-sized pieces. Layer in the dish with the peas, carrots, cheese and peaches. Mix the peach juice with the undiluted soup and pour over the contents of the dish. Crush the potato crisps and sprinkle on the top. Cover with foil and bake in the oven for 45 minutes. Uncover and brown under the grill or in the oven.
   Excellent served with jacket potatoes or plain boiled rice.

Turkey Divan

From Miss Abigail Mottram, Wellow, Isle of Wight

This recipe was given to my grandmother by my godmother.

Serves 4

1 × 9-oz (250-g) pack fresh or frozen broccoli
3 tablespoons grated Parmesan or Cheddar cheese
12 oz (350 g) cooked turkey or chicken

For the cream sauce
3 tablespoons butter
3 tablespoons flour or cornflour
½ pint (300 ml) milk
1 chicken stock cube
¼ pint (150 ml) single cream
2–3 tablespoons medium dry sherry
2 egg yolks
2 tablespoons thick or whipped cream or yoghurt
Salt
Freshly ground black pepper

Pre-heat the oven to 350°F (180°C), gas mark 4.

Arrange the broccoli around an ovenproof dish and sprinkle with half the cheese. Make the cream sauce by whisking together the butter, flour, milk and chicken stock cube over a low heat until the sauce thickens. Stir in the cream, sherry, egg yolks and cream or yoghurt, but do not allow the mixture to boil. Season to taste with salt and freshly ground black pepper. Spoon half the cream sauce over the broccoli. Add the turkey or chicken, chopped, if wished. Spoon the rest of the sauce over and sprinkle with the remaining cheese. Bake in the oven for about 30 minutes until golden brown.

Santa's Trifle ○

From Mrs B. Armstrong, Manchester

An excellent way of using left-over Christmas pudding.

Serves 4

8 oz (225 g) Christmas pudding
Finely grated rind and juice of 1
* orange*
1 tablespoon brandy or sherry

½ pint (300 ml) custard
¼ pint (150 ml) double cream,
* whipped*
A few whole hazelnuts

Break up the Christmas pudding with a fork. Add the juice and rind of the orange and the brandy, and mix well. Half fill individual serving glasses with the mixture, pour on the custard and allow to cool. Decorate with piped cream and hazelnuts.

For children: Make a Santa's face using glacé cherries for the mouth, angelica for the eyebrows and nose, and hazelnuts for the eyes.

❀ TWELFTH NIGHT (5/6 JANUARY) ❀

Twelfth Night sees the end of the Twelve Days of Christmas and since the fourth century it has marked the start of the Feast of Epiphany. It seems there is some debate about when Twelfth Night occurs. Today, it is generally considered to be on the night of 6 January, but at one time Twelfth Night referred to the evening of 5 January and some still insist on this date.

Traditionally Twelfth Night was an occasion for games, feasting and merriment, bringing the Christmas festivities to a fitting conclusion. Today it is a time for taking down the Christmas tree and packing away the decorations for next year. In medieval times there would have been games of forfeit and revelry. In the Tudor period masques or plays were very popular and Shakespeare's *Twelfth Night* was probably written for such a celebration at court, in 1601.

An essential feature of these celebrations was the Twelfth Night Cake, which continued in popularity into the late nineteenth century, when it was upstaged by the Christmas Cake. Traditionally, a bean was cooked in the cake and whoever found it was crowned 'King of the Bean' for the evening.

Twelfth Night Cake

From Mrs Norah Wood, Eastbourne, East Sussex

The principal decoration for the cake should be twelve candles and stars. A blue-coloured icing suggestive of a clear sky assists in carrying out the scheme for the 'Feast of the Star'.

Makes 1 × 8-in (20-cm) cake

8 oz (225 g) flour	2 oz (50 g) glacé cherries
1 teaspoon mixed spice	8 oz (225 g) butter
6 oz (175 g) currants	8 oz (225 g) sugar
8 oz (225 g) sultanas	4 eggs
2 oz (50 g) chopped mixed peel	A little milk to mix

Pre-heat the oven to 350°F (180°C), gas mark 4.

Grease a cake tin and line with paper. Sieve the flour and spice into a bowl, and mix in the fruit. Cream the butter and sugar together, then beat in the eggs one at a time. Stir in the flour and fruit mixture alternately with the milk, adding a little of each at a time. Blend all the ingredients together; put into the prepared tin and bake in a moderate oven for 2 hours.

✵ EPIPHANY (6 JANUARY) ✵

Epiphany came from the Greek word meaning 'manifestation' and it commemorates God's presence in the world through the manifestation of His Son, Jesus Christ. Originally four manifestations were celebrated:

His appearance to the shepherds,
'. . . the Shepherds said to one another, "Let's go to Bethlehem and see this thing that has happened, which the Lord has told us about."'
(Luke 2 : 15)

His appearance to the Three Kings or Wise Men,
'. . . On coming to the house, they saw the child with his mother Mary, and they bowed down and worshipped him. Then they opened their treasures and presented him with gifts of gold and of frankincense and of myrrh.'
(Matthew 2 : 11)

At his baptism,
'At that time Jesus came from Nazareth in Galilee and was baptised by John in the Jordan. As Jesus was coming up out of the water, he saw heaven being torn open and the Spirit descending on him like a dove.'
(Mark 1 : 9 & 10)

And at his first miracle at the wedding in Cana, where he turned water into wine,
'. . . the master of the banquet tasted the water that had been turned into wine. He did not realise where it had come from, though the servants who had drawn the water knew.'
(John 2 : 9)

This festival was celebrated by the early Church long before Christmas and even today the Eastern Orthodox Church regards it as more important. In the Armenian Church 6 January is observed as Christmas Day.

Since Western Christians adopted this festival in the fourth century it has gradually focused more on the Wise Men, known as the Adoration of the Magi, as they represented Gentiles of all races and nations.

Ever since the eleventh century, on 6 January British monarchs have re-enacted a symbolic bringing of gifts to the Christ child. Today this takes place in the Chapel Royal, St James's Palace, London and the monarch is represented by members of the Royal household. As the ushers approach the altar with the Queen's offering, they bow three times in memory of the Three Kings. The offering is received by the Bishop of London and as the ushers retire they again bow three times. The gold is represented by twenty-five sovereigns and their equivalent value is donated to charity.

Shepherd's Pie Fit for Kings

From Josephine Perrott, Burgess Hill, Sussex

I regularly prepare this for my family because it is not complicated, not too time-consuming and it's extremely nutritious.

Serves 4

4 lb (1.75 kg) potatoes	2 onions, chopped
2 oz (50 g) margarine	3 cloves garlic, chopped
2 tablespoons milk	1 × 11-oz (300-g) tin condensed
1½ lb (750 g) minced beef	tomato soup
4 leeks	1 beef stock cube, crumbled

Pre-heat the oven to 425°F (220°C), gas mark 7.

Peel and cut the potatoes into about 40 medium-sized pieces. Boil until soft and save the water to add to the pie later. Mash the potatoes with the margarine and milk. Fry the mince gently in its own fat until brown. Continue cooking the mince gently for about 10 minutes until tender. While the mince and potatoes are cooking, wash, trim and cut the leeks into 1-in (2.5-cm) lengths. Bring the leeks to the boil in salted water, then drain. Put the leeks into a deep 10×12-in (25×30-cm) baking tin with about 1½ pints (900 ml) of stock or water (from the boiled potatoes). Add the onions, garlic, soup and stock cube and stir well. Drain the fat from the mince, then add to the mixture in the baking tin. Stir well. Cover with the mashed potatoes and score with a fork. Put into the top half of the oven for about 1 hour or until the potato is golden brown.

Delicious served with seasonal vegetables and gravy.

The Wise Men's Cake

From Catherine O'Neill, East Grinstead, West Sussex

I am French and after nine years spent in this country, there is one custom I still miss, called 'La Galette des Rois'. An appropriate translation could be 'The Wise Men's Cake'. It is a cake baked by all French bakers and patissiers for the festival of Epiphany. This cake is baked and sold, decorated with a golden paper crown to symbolise the gifts brought by the Wise Men to Mary and Jesus. The crown is then given to whoever discovers the broad bean which is hidden in the cake. Modern times have meant that little plastic figures have replaced the broad bean, but . . . the tradition remains.

Makes 1×7-in (18-cm) cake

9 oz (250 g) flour
2 teaspoons salt
3 oz (75 g) unsalted butter, cut into
* pieces*
1 very fresh egg

6 fl oz (175 ml) water
4½ oz (120 g) unsalted butter, cut
* into pieces*
1 egg white

Sieve the flour, make a well in the centre and add the salt, 3 oz (75 g) butter, egg and water. Mix together well until all the ingredients are well incorporated. Do not be afraid to knead the dough until this is achieved. Let the dough stand for 40 minutes. After this, add the remaining butter and work as for puff pastry. Pre-heat the oven to 350°F (180°C), gas mark 4. Let the dough stand for another 10 minutes and then roll out the dough in a circle shape, 1-in (2.5-cm) thick. Put on to a baking sheet or in a round cake tin and glaze with the egg white. Let it stand for 15 minutes. Finally, put into a moderate oven and bake until it is nice and golden.

Crown Cake

From Mrs G. S. Moynihan, Alton, Hampshire

This spectacular Norwegian 'Kransekake' is often baked for special occasions such as confirmations and weddings.

Makes 1 × 10-in (25-cm) cake

1 lb (450 g) ground sweet almonds
About 25 ground bitter almonds
1 lb (450 g) icing sugar
3 egg whites
For the icing
3 oz (75 g) icing sugar
½ egg white
½ teaspoon lemon juice

To decorate
Miniature crackers
Marzipan flowers
Sweets
Flag

Pre-heat the oven to 300°F (150°C), gas mark 2.
Mix together the ground almonds and the icing sugar. Add 1 egg white. Set the mixture over a low heat until it is tepid, then mix in the other 2 egg whites, one at a time. Press the mixture through a fluted nozzle, about ½-in (1-cm) in diameter. The paste should be piped in separate rings on to a greased baking tray, the diameter of the largest ring should be about 10 in (25 cm) and each subsequent ring must be ¼ in (5 mm) less in diameter down to the last at 2 in (5 cm) in diameter. Bake in a cool oven until light golden brown. Remove the rings and while still warm, mount one ring on top of the other, making a tower or crown, the largest ring forming the base. Mix the icing ingredients together thoroughly and decorate the cake by piping a thin line of white glacé icing in zig-zag lines all over the cake in an irregular design. Miniature crackers, marzipan flowers or sweets are fixed to the sides with lightly browned caramel. The crown is topped by a small national flag or with artificial or marzipan flowers.

❀ WINTER SUNDAY LUNCHES ❀

Steak and Kidney Pudding ○

From Mrs E. Jones, Burton Joyce, Nottingham

This is a real winter warmer, and a very useful dish to put into the oven while you are at church or out for the day.

Makes 1 × 2-pint (1.2-litre) pudding

1 lb (450 g) stewing steak
4 oz (100 g) ox kidney
1 tablespoon plain flour
Salt and pepper

8 oz (225 g) self-raising flour
4 oz (100 g) shredded suet
A little cold water

Trim and cut the stewing steak into cubes and cut the kidney into small pieces. Roll in seasoned plain flour. To make the crust, mix the flour, suet and salt and add enough cold water to make a stiff consistency. Grease a 2-pint (1.2-l) pudding basin. Roll out the dough, keeping back sufficient for the lid, and line the basin. Put in the steak and kidney. Add a teacupful of cold water. Cover with the remaining dough and seal the edges well. Cover the pudding with greased greaseproof paper, then with a second piece of greaseproof paper and secure with string. Steam for at least 3 hours, but the pudding can be left steaming for much longer. Make sure you use a large enough pan so that it does not boil dry.

Steamed Ginger Pudding ◯

From Ann Langley, Tunbridge Wells, Kent

My grandfather was organist to the Duke and Duchess of Portland at Welbeck Abbey and he looked beautiful in his scarlet cassock crossing the altar to the organ. We all obviously attended church and this pudding could be left steaming with impunity, being further improved by steaming for over 2 hours! Still a favourite with my grandchildren.

Serves 4

2 oz (50 g) white breadcrumbs
4 oz (100 g) self-raising flour
4 oz (100 g) suet, chopped
6 oz (175 g) demerara sugar
1 teaspoon ground ginger (or to taste)

1 teaspoon bicarbonate of soda
1 egg, beaten, with enough milk to make up to 8 fl oz (250 ml)
1 rounded tablespoon golden syrup

Grease a 3-pint (1.75-l) pudding basin, as the pudding needs room for expansion. Mix all the ingredients together. The mixture should be very sloppy, so add more milk if it is too dry. Pour into the basin and cover with greased foil or greaseproof paper. Steam for 2 hours, or longer if preferred, making sure that it does not boil dry. The pudding should be very light and a lovely golden brown.

Served with warmed golden syrup, cream or custard, this makes a delicious traditional dessert.

❧ CHURCH AND FAMILY SUPPERS ❧

Suppers are a feature of church life in Britain enjoyed by many and they are a marvellous way of bringing the church family together. The harvest supper is the most popular, but these meals now take place throughout the rest of the year too. Here are some good ideas for cold winter evenings, but they can be eaten at any time. Many of these dishes would also be good for family suppers following the Sunday evening service.

Alan Titchmarsh's Mince and Spaghetti Savoury

This is one of my favourite recipes. It is a really terrific meal – a sort of combination of sweet and savoury. It was made by my landlady at Kew Gardens when I was a student there and she used to serve it up in the evening with a glass of red wine, if I was lucky. I don't know whether the plants in my care grew very well, but I did!

Serves 6

1 lb (450 g) mince
1 onion, chopped
1 clove garlic
1 oz (25 g) sultanas
½ teaspoon mixed herbs
A pinch of nutmeg
1 tablespoon brown sugar
1×8-oz (225-g) tin tomatoes
1 tablespoon flour
Stock or water
8 oz (225 g) spaghetti

For the cheese sauce
2 oz (50 g) butter
2 oz (50 g) flour
1 pint (600 ml) milk
4 oz (100 g) Cheddar cheese, grated
2 dessertspoons vinegar

Pre-heat the oven to 350°F (180°C), gas mark 4.

Fry the mince, onion, garlic, sultanas, herbs, nutmeg, sugar and tomatoes until browned. Thicken with the flour. Moisten with a little stock or water, if necessary, but leave quite firm. Put in a 2-pint (1.2-l) pie dish. Boil the spaghetti in salted water until just cooked, then drain.

To make the cheese sauce, cook the butter, flour and milk over a low heat, stirring continuously, until the mixture thickens. Cook for 3 minutes, then add the cheese and vinegar. Put the spaghetti on top of the mince. Pour the cheese sauce over the spaghetti and cook for 30 minutes.

Serve immediately with a glass of red wine.

Bonnie's Pizza Recipe ○

From John Newbury, Editor, Good Morning Sunday

My wife and I were given this recipe by a woman in the United States, who was a friend of a friend. We turned up on her doorstep as total strangers and Bonnie and her family took us in as one of their own. The pizza is not only marvellous to taste but also, every time I eat it, allows me to re-taste the memories of a very happy holiday with lovely folk. We have found it first to disappear at church suppers!

Makes 2×10-in (25-cm) pies or 12×5-in (13-cm) pies

For the sauce
1×1¾-lb (750-g) can tomatoes, sieved
2 tablespoons tomato purée or ketchup
2 large onions, diced
1 clove garlic
1 teaspoon oregano
½ teaspoon salt
¼ teaspoon pepper
1 teaspoon parsley

For the crust
1 oz (25 g) fresh yeast or ½ oz (15 g) dried yeast
½ pint (300 ml) warm water
2 teaspoons sugar
1 lb (450 g) plain flour
1 teaspoon cooking oil
1½ teaspoons salt

4 oz (100 g) Cheddar cheese, grated

Put all the sauce ingredients into a saucepan and cook on a low heat for ½ an hour until thick.

To make the crust, soften the yeast in the warm water, add the sugar, and stir until dissolved. Add half the flour and beat until well blended. Mix in the oil and salt. Stir in the remaining flour. Turn on to a floured board and knead until smooth, about 5 to 10 minutes. Oil a large bowl, preferably with a snap-on lid. Place the dough in the bowl and turn it to cover it with oil. Cover with the lid or a damp cloth (to stop a crust forming on the dough). Leave to rise until it has doubled in size. Knead down and put in the refrigerator until it stops growing (you will need to knead it down several times before it stops – watch out! It may take over your fridge!).

Take the dough from the fridge ½ an hour before it is wanted, and leave it to stand and soften. Pre-heat the oven to 425°F (220°C), gas mark 7. Grease a baking tray and spread the dough over it thinly. Then spread the sauce on top. Cooked meat or vegetables may be added if desired. Top with grated cheese and cook in a hot oven for 15 to 20 minutes.

This may seem a lot of trouble to go to but the dough and sauce will keep for about 10 days in the fridge so once it is made up it is a quick dish to make for suppers. Keep the dough covered at all times until used, to prevent a crust forming.

Thora Hird's Spaghetti Bake

When I used to come home late after the theatre the last thing I felt like was eating. But Scottie, my husband, felt that I should eat a good solid meal and so he invented this dish to tempt me, and it has been a great favourite of mine ever since. The delicious smell of Spaghetti Bake, lovingly prepared for me by Scottie, never failed to win me over, much to his delight.

Serves 2

2 large onions, peeled and sliced
2 oz (50 g) butter
Salt and pepper
Sage or mixed herbs
3 oz (75 g) long spaghetti

2 × 14-oz (400-g) tins peeled
* tomatoes*
6 oz (175 g) strong Cheddar cheese,
* grated*
Sprigs of parsley to garnish

Pre-heat the oven to 300°F (150°C), gas mark 2.
Fry the onions in the melted butter until tender and pale golden brown. Arrange in an ovenproof dish and season with salt, pepper and herbs. Break the dry spaghetti into 3-in (7.5-cm) lengths and scatter over the onions.
   Pour the contents of the tins of tomatoes over the spaghetti, cutting them up if necessary. Arrange the grated cheese in an even layer over the top. Cover with kitchen foil or a lid and bake in a cool oven for 1¼ hours. Remove the foil or lid and return to a moderately hot oven at 375°F (190°C), gas mark 5 for 10 to 15 minutes, or until golden brown. Garnish with parsley and serve at once.

Richard Stilgoe's Kind Hearts and Coronets

Isn't it interesting which bits of a body people will eat? Everyone likes legs and ribs. No-one seems to mind rump. But hearts have peculiar connotations, based entirely on medieval superstitions. If you can get over this, they are delicious and very cheap.

Serves 4

5 large firm tomatoes
1 teaspoon sugar
Salt
Ground black pepper
Basil
4 large or 8 small lamb's hearts

For the stuffing
2 oz (50 g) shredded suet
2 oz (50 g) bacon, diced
4 oz (100 g) stale bread, grated
2 teaspoons parsley, chopped
½ teaspoon mixed herbs
Grated rind of ½ lemon
Salt and pepper
1 egg, beaten

Pre-heat the oven to 350°F (180°C), gas mark 4.

Cut the tomatoes around the equator in a zig-zag pattern. The tomatoes should then separate into 2 halves (there are 5 tomatoes because 1 of them is bound to go wrong). Sprinkle them with the sugar, salt, ground pepper and basil and leave in the refrigerator for a few hours. Mix all the stuffing ingredients together thoroughly.

Wash the hearts and cut out the insides to leave 1 clean cavity in each heart. Stuff with the stuffing. Put the hearts into a hot fatty (or oily) roasting tin. Baste. Bake in the oven for 1 hour, or until the hearts are well cooked and the top of the stuffing is crispy. Serve these tasty hearts with the tomatoes, and things like potato crisps, cos lettuce, radishes and raw onion rings.

Jacob's Mince Special
(Recipe tested and approved by Roger Royle)

From Tanya Astley, Production Assistant, Good Morning Sunday

I recommend this recipe as you can enjoy a splendid, filling meal for just a few pounds, and it is very easy to make. We read in the Bible that Jacob beat his brother Esau into presenting his father with a hot meal. I like to imagine it was something similar to this dish.

Serves 4

1 lb (450 g) minced beef	*Salt and pepper*
1 onion, chopped	*Bisto granules*
4 oz (100 g) mushrooms, chopped	*8 oz (225 g) frozen mixed vegetables*
1 tablespoon tomato purée	*1 lb (450 g) potatoes*
Mixed herbs	

Aim the mince for the frying pan. Allow it to smoulder in its own fat. Just before it looks as if it's going to burn add the chopped onion and mushrooms. Once this looks nearly edible add the spoonful of tomato purée and stir. Add as much herbs and seasoning as you like. For the best gravy in the world boil the kettle (i.e. boil the water in the kettle) and make the Bisto granule gravy – just one mug full and make it nice and thick – so you can just about stir it! Spoon out (!) the gravy into a saucepan and add the contents of the frying pan. Cook at a sensible heat – below boiling point.

Boil yet another kettle of water, then pour the water into a saucepan and bung in the vegetables. Let them boil, then once a bit soggy, strain them and add to the mincemeat saucepan. Let it cook gently for about 30 minutes and whilst waiting cook yourself some yummy mashed potatoes. At a price I'll let you into the secret recipe.

Lay the table, dish out the food, then after saying 'grace' enjoy a delicious meal. If you've made too much, ring me and I'll come and eat it with you.

Kenneth McKellar's Chäs-Schnitte (Swiss après-ski dish)

This recipe is dear to all our family. My wife, who is Swiss, introduced me to it and now 'the man of the house' can gain brownie points by preparing it fairly quickly, particularly on a cold evening after a bracing walk. 'Chäs-schnitte' literally means 'cheese slice' but as you see, there's a lot more to it than that.

Serves 1

1 small round flameproof dish
1 slice rye or wholemeal bread
1 tablespoon dry white wine
1 slice gammon or cured ham

2–3 slices of Gruyère cheese
1 egg
Salt and black pepper or paprika

Put a slice of bread into a small round flameproof dish which has been warmed. Pour the wine over it. Place the ham on top. Put under a hot grill for a couple of minutes. Remove, and sprinkle on the Gruyère cheese. Place under the grill until the cheese sizzles. Meanwhile, fry the egg sunny-side up in a minimum of oil and slide on top of the bubbling cheese. Replace under the grill for a couple of minutes till the egg is slightly crisp round the edges. Remove the dish and sprinkle with salt and black pepper. Serve on a wooden board.

Have a glass of dry white wine with this tasty dish and think of the ski slopes!

Mary O'Hara's Baked Bean Recipe

One of my favourite recipes and a perfect dish to fall back on if you've a million and one other things to do at the same time.

Serves 2

1×1-lb (450-g) tin baked beans
(without tomato sauce)
1 tablespoon brown sugar
1 small onion

A pinch of dry mustard
A dash of Worcestershire sauce
2 rashers bacon, chopped or whole
2 slices cheese

Simply empty the contents of the tin into a saucepan. Add the other ingredients. Place on a very low heat and leave to cook gently until all the ingredients have blended. A little beer may be added to the recipe during the cooking.

Tasty served with fresh granary or wholemeal bread.

2

Spring

❦ COLLOP MONDAY ❦

This is the name generally given to the Monday before the start of Lent on Ash Wednesday. The word 'collop' is Scandinavian, meaning a slice of meat. In medieval times the Lenten fast was extremely strict, so the days preceding Ash Wednesday were the last opportunity to eat certain 'luxury' foods not allowed during the forty days of fasting. Monday was traditionally the day for finishing the meat and the main meal usually consisted of rashers of bacon or meat collops and eggs – hence the name. In Cornwall they preferred Pea Soup, so they called the day 'Peason Monday'.

Minced Collops

From Sue Goodman, Castle Bromwich, Birmingham

There are numerous recipes for collops. This one, from Scotland, uses beef.

Serves 4

1 oz (25 g) dripping
2 onions, peeled and finely chopped
1 lb (450 g) minced beef
Salt and black pepper

1–2 pints (600–1200 ml) water or
  beef stock
4 eggs
4 slices hot toast

Melt the dripping in a heavy based saucepan and fry the onions over a low heat for about 5 minutes or until soft. Add the minced beef, cover with a lid and fry until the beef is browned and has separated into grains. Season to taste with salt and freshly ground pepper. Pour over the water or stock until the meat is almost covered. Then put the lid on the pan and simmer the contents for 45 minutes. Stir occasionally and take the lid off the pan towards the end of the cooking time. When the meat is cooked, the liquid should have almost evaporated. Poach the eggs. Spoon the meat on to slices of hot toast and top each portion with a poached egg. The minced collops could also be served with creamed potatoes instead of toast.

❀ SHROVE TUESDAY ❀

Shrove Tuesday is the last day before Lent, which begins on Ash Wednesday. The word 'shrove' comes from the Old English 'shrivan', meaning 'to shrive' or 'to absolve', as this was the day of the one time compulsory pre-Lent confessions or 'shrifts'.

Shrove Tuesday was the last day for using up all the fat, butter and eggs before the Lenten fast, so pancakes were traditionally made, as they still are today – hence the nickname 'pancake day'! In parts of northern England or Scotland it is often known as Fastern's or Fassern's Eve, because it is the day before the fast.

Traditionally this has been a day for fun, feasting and pranks before the long period of self-denial and self-discipline. The pancake race is a custom that still survives, one at Olney in Buckinghamshire dates back to 1445. Shrovetide football games were also popular, and these were usually a mass free-for-all with few rules. Probably the oldest of these games is one played at Atherstone near the Warwickshire border, which is said to have started during the reign of King John.

Jenny's Basic Pancake Recipe

From Jenny Pitt, Production Assistant, Good Morning Sunday

Makes 8 to 10 pancakes

4 oz (100 g) plain flour
½ teaspoon of salt
1 egg

½ pint (300 ml) milk
Sugar or lemon to flavour

Sieve the flour and salt into a bowl. Make a well in the centre of the mixture. Add the egg and a little of the milk. Beat well. Add the rest of the milk, still beating. A little water should be added if the batter is too thick. Put some fat in the frying pan and heat on a medium heat until a tiny piece of batter sizzles and floats in the fat. For each pancake, pour enough batter to coat the bottom of the pan thinly, rolling the pan to spread the batter properly. Cook until golden brown on the bottom. With great manual dexterity, toss the pancake to within inches of the ceiling. Ensure that the frying pan is positioned to allow the pancake to drop neatly back into it. Cook the other side. Remove the pancake from the pan. Lightly sprinkle with sugar or lemon to taste, and then fold and eat.

Anna Wing's
Cottage Cheese Pancakes

These are very popular with children and are both tasty and nutritious, and
they are ideal for a Sunday breakfast or a tea-time treat.

Serves 4

6 medium-sized eggs, separated
3 oz (75 g) white flour
2 tablespoons sugar
1 teaspoon salt
A pinch of cinnamon

1 × 10-oz (275-g) carton cottage
  cheese
⅛ teaspoon of cream of tartar
Oil for frying

Combine the egg yolks, flour, sugar, salt, cinnamon and cottage cheese in a
blender or food processor. Combine the egg whites and cream of tartar and
beat until stiff, but not dry. Fold the beaten whites into the cheese batter.
Oil the frying pan and heat until the oil is hot but not smoking. Pour in
sufficient batter to make a pancake about 4 in (10 cm) in diameter. Fry until
golden on both sides. Serve at once with lemon and brown sugar.

Crêpes aux Cerises

From Ruth Maltby, London, SW3

Serves 4

Enriched pancake batter (see page 50)

For the filling
  8 oz (225 g) black cherries (fresh or
    tinned)
  1 tablespoon kirsch

For the topping
  Caster sugar for dusting
  About 3 fl oz (85 ml) double cream
  A pinch of ground cinnamon
  2 tablespoons almonds, browned
    and chopped

Pre-heat the oven to 400°F (200°C), gas mark 6.
  Make the pancakes. Stone the cherries, and pour the kirsch over them. Put a
tablespoon of cherries on each pancake. Roll up the pancakes, place on a
baking sheet and dust well with caster sugar. Heat through in the oven for 3
to 4 minutes. Place in a hot serving dish. Boil the cream with the cinnamon,
pour this over the pancakes and scatter the almonds on top. Serve at once.

Roger Royle's Spinach Pancakes

Serves 4

First you have to make 12 pancakes. Well, there is no need for me to tell you how to do those because that is spelt out for you on page 48. But I shall tell you about the filling. You need:

1 lb (450 g) fresh spinach or a
1 × 12-oz (350-g) pack of frozen
spinach
1½ oz (40 g) butter
1½ oz (40 g) flour

1 pint (600 ml) milk
Salt
Freshly milled pepper
4 oz (100 g) Gruyère cheese, grated

Pre-heat the oven to 400°F (200°C), gas mark 6.

Have your pancakes prepared and hot. If you are using fresh spinach, wash it well and remove the rib from the leaves. I am lazy – I always use frozen spinach. Cook in a covered saucepan over moderate heat for about 10 to 15 minutes, without adding water. Drain well and chop finely. If you are using frozen spinach then just follow the instructions on the pack. Melt the butter in the saucepan over a low heat and stir in the flour. Do this very thoroughly otherwise you get lumps. Cook gently for a moment, then gradually stir in half the milk, beating well all the time to make a thick sauce. Once again, keep an eye open for lumps. Bring to the boil and cook gently for 2 to 3 minutes. Season with salt and pepper and stir in all but 1 oz (25 g) of the cheese. Stir about half this sauce into the spinach purée. Fill the pancakes with the mixture, roll up and place in a buttered serving dish. Thin down the remaining sauce with the rest of the milk to make a coating consistency. Check the seasoning again and then pour the sauce over the pancakes. Sprinkle with the remaining cheese and brown well in a hot oven for about 10 minutes. Serve hot. You can't go wrong.

Enriched Pancake Batter

From Ruth Maltby, London, SW3

Makes 8 to 10 pancakes

4 oz (100 g) plain flour
A pinch of salt
1 egg
1 egg yolk

½ pint (300 ml) milk
1 tablespoon melted butter or olive oil

Sift the flour with the salt into a mixing bowl. Make a well in the centre, add the egg and yolk and begin to add the milk, stirring all the time. When half the milk has been added, stir in the melted butter or oil and beat well until smooth. Add the remaining milk. Cover and leave to stand for ½ an hour before using. Heat a heavy 6-in (15-cm) frying pan and make the pancakes. Slide the pancakes on to a wire cake rack. Stack them one on top of the other and keep in a clean tea towel until wanted. Allow 2 pancakes per person.

To re-heat the pancakes pre-heat the oven to 400°F (200°C), gas mark 6. Melt about 1 oz (25 g) of butter and brush it over a baking sheet. Lay the pancakes over, lapping along the sheet. Brush with more melted butter to exclude the air and protect the pancakes during cooking. Put the baking sheet into the oven for 3 to 4 minutes.

For pancakes with a stuffing, stuff them when cold and to re-heat bake them as above (brushed with melted butter) for 7 to 10 minutes.

To deep-freeze cooked pancakes stack them one on top of the other with a piece of greaseproof or waxed paper between each layer, then wrap in foil or a polythene bag.

Lenten Biscuits

From Mrs Jean Darby, Amblecote, Stourbridge

In the Middle Ages these biscuits were enjoyed on Shrove Tuesday as a special treat on the last day of rich eating before the Lenten fast.

Makes about 24 biscuits

4 oz (100 g) butter or margarine	*1 oz (25 g) chopped mixed peel*
4 oz (100 g) caster sugar	*A pinch of mixed spice (optional)*
1 egg yolk	*Milk to mix*
8 oz (225 g) plain flour	*Egg white for glazing*
2 oz (50 g) currants	*Caster sugar for glazing*

Pre-heat the oven to 325°F (160°C), gas mark 3.

Cream the butter and sugar together until fluffy. Beat in the egg yolk. Fold in the flour, currants and mixed peel, mixing well. Add the mixed spice, if liked. Add the milk a little at a time, until the mixture forms a stiff dough. Roll the dough out to about ⅛ in (3 mm) thick and cut out in 2-in (5-cm) rounds. Arrange on a greased baking tray and bake for 15 to 20 minutes. After 10 minutes in the oven, brush the biscuits quickly with egg white and sprinkle with caster sugar. Return to the oven for a further 5 to 10 minutes. Cool on a wire rack.

✧ LENT ✧

Lent begins on Ash Wednesday and is a forty-day period of fasting in preparation for Easter, commemorating the forty days Jesus spent in the wilderness. The name is derived from the Old English 'lencten', meaning spring.

In medieval Britain the Lenten fast was strictly adhered to as much out of practical necessity as religious duty. At this time of year the winter stocks were running out, meat was scarce and it was a long wait for the harvest. So Henry VIII and subsequently the Puritans, enforced abstention quite strictly – no meat or dairy produce were allowed.

Today most people do not fast, but many try to 'give up something for Lent' such as chocolate, cigarettes or alcohol.

Lent is a time to think of others and nowadays many societies organise 'hunger lunches' which consist of only soup, bread or cheese, and the money saved goes to feed the starving.

Kent Lent Pie

From Mrs Eileen Walker, Hurstpierpoint, Hassocks, West Sussex

Serves 4 to 6

8 oz (225 g) shortcrust pastry　　　*2 eggs*
½ pint (300 ml) milk　　　*Rind of 1 lemon*
1 oz (25 g) ground rice　　　*Pinch of salt*
2 oz (50 g) butter　　　*¼ teaspoon ground nutmeg*
2 oz (50 g) sugar　　　*1 oz (25 g) currants*

Pre-heat the oven to 375°F (190°C), gas mark 5.

Use the pastry to line an 8-in (20-cm) flan ring and bake blind for 15 minutes. Remove from the oven and leave to cool. Put the milk and ground rice in a saucepan and bring to the boil, stirring continuously until the mixture thickens. Allow to cool. Cream the butter and sugar until pale and fluffy. Beat in the eggs one at a time. Grate in the lemon rind and salt, nutmeg and rice mixture. Pour into the flan case, and sprinkle the currants on top. Bake in the centre of the oven for 35 to 40 minutes until firm to the touch and golden. Serve warm.

Overnight Cake

From Mrs Alison Willis, Hartley Wintney, Hampshire

This recipe has been in use in my family since early war times! In hard times of shortage of ingredients it served for Christmas and birthday cakes – but in these more affluent times I would suggest it might be used in Lent as it has no eggs! A busy mum can quickly mix it up late in the evening if desired, and bake the next day – thus justifying its name of Overnight Cake.

Makes 1×8-in (20-cm) cake

8 oz (225 g) self-raising flour
A pinch of salt
1 teaspoon bicarbonate of soda
1 teaspoon nutmeg
1 teaspoon spice

2 oz (50 g) margarine
8 oz (225 g) mixed cake fruit (or up
to 12 oz (350 g) if desired)
4 oz (100 g) dark brown sugar
1 breakfast cup of milk

Sieve the flour, salt, bicarbonate of soda and spices together. Rub in the margarine until the mixture resembles fine breadcrumbs. Add the fruit and sugar and mix all the ingredients together with the milk. Cover and leave overnight. Pre-heat the oven to 350°F (180°C), gas mark 4. Turn the mixture into a greased and floured 8-in (20-cm) cake tin. Bake in a moderately hot oven for 1¾ hours.

Moist Coconut and Carrot Cake

From Mrs Janenne Mills, Chasetown, Staffordshire

There is no fat in this recipe so this is very good during Lent.

Makes 1×8-in (20-cm) cake

12 oz (350 g) wholemeal self-raising
flour
2 teaspoons cinnamon
8 oz (225 g) light soft brown sugar
12 oz (350 g) carrots, peeled and
coarsely grated

2 oz (50 g) desiccated coconut
7 fl oz (200 ml) oil
5 tablespoons milk
3 medium eggs, beaten
Icing sugar to dust

Pre-heat the oven to 350°F (180°C), gas mark 4.
Mix together the flour, cinnamon, sugar, carrot and coconut in a large bowl. Stir in the oil, milk and eggs and mix well. Turn into an 8-in (20-cm) loose-bottomed deep cake tin, which has been greased, lined and greased again, and bake for 1½ hours until firm. Leave in the tin to cool, turn out on to a wire rack, and sprinkle the top with icing sugar.

❦ ST DAVID'S DAY (1 MARCH) ❦

St David or Dewi is the patron saint of Wales and 1 March is the Welsh national day. David was a sixth-century abbot-bishop and he founded many monastic communities, the most famous of which was at St David's, Pembrokeshire, where the regime was very strict. During the twelfth century his shrine became an important centre of pilgrimage.

The Welsh national emblems are the leek and the daffodil, but it seems there is no satisfactory explanation as to why this is so. However, one theory about the origin of the leek as a national symbol refers to a battle in the sixth century between the Welshmen and Saxons. David suggested that the Welsh wear a leek in their caps so that they could recognise one another, otherwise they were in danger of killing each other as well as the enemy. Another theory suggests that in the same battle it was David who wore a leek in his cap so that he stood out in the battle when he led the Welsh to victory against the Saxons.

Richard Adams' Welsh Rarebit

If desired, a poached egg can be placed on top of the Rarebit by way of a variation.

Serves 2

3 oz (75 g) Cheddar cheese, grated　*A few drops of soy sauce*
Salt and pepper　*A little milk*
Dry mustard　*2 slices of toast*

Season the grated cheese with salt, pepper and dry mustard to taste. Add a few drops of soy sauce and enough milk to mix the ingredients into a stiff paste. Spread the mixture on to 2 freshly-made pieces of toast and brown under the grill. Serve immediately.

Sir Harry Secombe's Welsh Cakes

This would go in the 'naughty but nice' section, if only you were having one! Very good after church on Sunday.

Makes about 18 cakes

1 lb (450 g) self-raising flour
A pinch of salt
4 oz (100 g) sugar
8 oz (225 g) butter or margarine, cut
  into pieces

8 oz (225 g) currants
1 egg
10–12 fl oz (300–350 ml) milk

Sift the flour, salt and sugar into a bowl, and rub in the butter with the fingertips until the mixture resembles fine breadcrumbs. Stir in the currants. Beat together the egg and milk, and pour them on to the dry ingredients. Mix with a knife until the mixture begins to bind together, then form into a ball with the fingertips. Turn out on to a lightly floured board and knead lightly until free from cracks. Roll out the mixture until about ¼ in (5 mm) thick and cut into 3-in (7.5-cm) rounds. Rub a griddle with a little lard and place over moderate heat to warm through. Transfer the cut mixture on to the griddle and cook until brown on the underside, then turn and leave for about 5 to 7 minutes until cooked through.
  Serve hot with butter.

Bara Claddu (Buttered Bun Loaf)

From Eirwen Gerrard, Whitchurch, Cardiff

Bara Claddu has been a great favourite with my family since the 1950s. I use the basic recipe but add chopped nuts and a tablespoon of golden syrup.

8 oz (225 g) flour
¼ teaspoon baking powder
8 oz (225 g) sugar
8 oz (225 g) dried mixed fruit

1 teaspoon mixed spice
1 egg, beaten
A little milk

Pre-heat the oven to 325°F (160°C), gas mark 3.
  Mix all the dry ingredients, then add the beaten egg and, if necessary, a little milk. Put into a greased loaf tin and bake in a moderate oven for about 1 hour. When cool, cut into slices, and serve well buttered.

❦ ST PATRICK'S DAY (17 MARCH) ❦

St Patrick is the patron saint of Ireland and his feast day is 17 March, which is the anniversary of his death and the Irish national holiday.

St Patrick lived in the fifth century and he was the son of a Roman tax collector, living in south-east Wales. As a boy he was captured by slave traders and taken to Ireland where he was sold. Six years later, he escaped to Gaul where he studied for the priesthood and then returned to Ireland as a missionary. Within ten years he had established churches all over Ireland. He died there in AD 461.

The Irish national emblem is the shamrock because, according to legend, St Patrick converted the pagan King Loigaire to Christianity by using the clover to demonstrate the mystery of the Holy Trinity. The Father, Son and Holy Ghost are united as one, and the clover has three separate leaves united in one stem.

Fine Textured Irish Wheaten Bread ○

From Mrs Frances Edwards, Thingwall, Wirral

Wheaten bread is traditionally made with buttermilk, but it is hard to come by in our area so, after a few failures, I came up with this recipe – my husband says that it is better than the farls we buy in Ireland.

I serve this bread with Salmon Pâté on St Patrick's Day.

Makes 4 farls

6 oz (175 g) plain white flour
½ teaspoon salt
1 teaspoon bicarbonate of soda
1 teaspoon cream of tartar
10 oz (275 g) wholemeal flour

1 × 5-oz (150-g) carton of plain
yoghurt, made up to ½ pint
(300 ml) with milk
1 oz (25 g) butter, melted

Pre-heat the oven to 425°F (220°C), gas mark 7.

Sieve the plain flour, salt, bicarbonate of soda and cream of tartar (making sure that there are no lumps in the soda). Add the wholemeal flour. Mix to a soft dough with the yoghurt and milk mixture (more or less liquid may be needed depending on the make of wholemeal flour). Lastly add the melted butter and mix well. Turn on to a floured surface, lightly knead and make into a flat round cake. Place on a floured baking sheet and mark into 4 farls. Bake in a hot oven for about 30 minutes, depending on the thickness of the farls. When it is cool, wrap in a clean cloth.

Brotchán Foltchep
(Traditional Leek and Oatmeal Soup)

From Frank Egan, Sunbury, Middlesex

For many centuries, oatmeal, milk and leeks were the staple diet of the Irish. Here they are combined to make a substantial soup. Legend has it that St Patrick tended a dying woman, who said that she had seen a herb in the air, and would die unless she ate it. St Patrick said to her: 'What is the semblance of the herb?' 'Like rushes,' saith the woman. Patrick blessed the rushes so that they became a leek. The woman ate it afterwards, and was whole at once. 'Brotchán' is the Irish for broth.

Serves 4

6 large leeks   *2 tablespoons flaked oatmeal*
2 pints (1.2 l) milk or stock   *Salt and pepper*
1 heaped tablespoon butter   *1 tablespoon chopped parsley*

Wash the leeks thoroughly to remove any grit. Leave on the green part and cut them into chunks about 1 in (2.5 cm) long. Heat up the liquid with the butter, and when boiling add the oatmeal. Allow to boil, then add the chopped leeks and season to taste. Cover and simmer gently for 45 minutes. Add the parsley and boil again for a few minutes.

For Nettle Brotchán use 4 cups of young nettle tops, packed tightly, instead of the leek and oatmeal. Wear gloves when picking them and cut with scissors. A little cream can be added, if liked.

❀ MOTHERING SUNDAY ❀

Mothering Sunday falls on the fourth Sunday in Lent and originally referred to the medieval requirement that the people and priest should visit the Mother Church, the cathedral of the diocese, on this day. The name could also be derived from the words of the Mass for this day where St Paul says, *'that Jerusalem above which is our Mother'*.

Years later, in the days when large households had live-in servants, the girls in service would be allowed home to visit their mothers. They would traditionally take a small gift, either a bunch of wild primroses or violets, or a simnel cake.

Today, many families go to special family services at church where the children collect small bunches of flowers for their mothers. Sons and daughters usually send a greeting card and give flowers or chocolates to their mothers.

All Saints' Melbourn Playgroup Cookies

From Rosemary Gatward, Melbourn, near Royston

The children in our playgroup make these cookies as gifts for their mothers every year.

Makes 16 to 20 biscuits

6 oz (175 g) plain flour
A pinch of salt
4 oz (100 g) butter or margarine
2 oz (50 g) caster sugar plus extra for
  dredging

A few drops of vanilla essence
1 egg white

Pre-heat the oven to 350°F (180°C), gas mark 4.
Sift the flour and salt into a large bowl. Rub in the fat until the mixture resembles fine breadcrumbs. Mix in 2 oz (50 g) sugar and the vanilla essence. Gather together to form a ball, then knead on a floured board until smooth. Roll out to ⅛–¼ in (3–5 mm) thick. Cut out the biscuits with a heart-shaped cutter and place on a greased baking tray. Beat the egg white with a fork, then brush each biscuit with egg white and sprinkle lightly with caster sugar. Bake in a moderate oven for 10 to 15 minutes until the biscuits are cooked and the topping crisp. We find they are best when only just cooked.

When cold, put the cookies in a bag, tie with a pink ribbon and give to your mother with much love on Mothering Sunday.

Wendy Craig's Old-fashioned Simnel Cake

Originally this cake was baked for Mothering Sunday, in the days when many girls went into service and Mothering Sunday was the one day in the year they were allowed home. It is now more usual to have Simnel Cake at Easter. There is an amusing legend about the name – some people say that a sister Nell and her brother Simon were going to make a cake for their mother. They had an argument as to whether to bake the cake or boil it (which was then quite a usual method of cooking a cake). In the end they made a baked and a boiled cake and stuck the two together, giving the characteristic division through the centre. The name of the cake was accordingly formed from their two names!

Makes 1×8-in (20-cm) cake or 2×6-in (15-cm) cakes

8 oz (225 g) butter
8 oz (225 g) soft light brown sugar
Finely grated rind of 1 lemon
4 eggs, beaten
8 oz (225 g) plain flour
½ teaspoon baking powder
½ teaspoon grated nutmeg
2 oz (50 g) cornflour

12 oz (350 g) mixed fruit
4 oz (100 g) glacé cherries, quartered
1 oz (25 g) ground almonds
1 lb (450 g) marzipan
To finish
2 tablespoons apricot jam, warmed
1 egg, beaten

Pre-heat the oven to 325°F (160°C), gas mark 3.
Cream the butter with the sugar and lemon rind until light and fluffy. Gradually beat in the eggs, beating well after each addition. Sift the flour with the baking powder, nutmeg and cornflour. Fold a third of the flour into the creamed mixture then fold in the fruit, cherries and ground almonds in two batches, alternating with the remaining flour. Spoon half the cake mixture into a greased and lined cake tin. Smooth the surface. Roll out the marzipan for the centre of the cake to a circle the size of the cake tin; use 8 oz (225 g) of the marzipan for the 8-in (20-cm) cake, or 4 oz (100 g) each for the 6-in (15-cm) cakes. Place the marzipan in the cake tin and top with the remaining cake mixture. Smooth the surface and make a hollow in the centre to help the cake to rise evenly. Bake the smaller cake for 1½ to 2 hours, or the larger for 2 to 2½ hours in the lower part of the oven, until the cake is golden brown, firm to the touch and no longer 'sings'. Leave to cool in the tin, turn out and remove the paper.
   At this stage I wrap the cake in greaseproof paper and store it for 3 to 4 weeks to mature in an air-tight container.

To finish for Mothering Sunday Brush the top of the cake with the warmed apricot jam. Roll out the remaining marzipan to a round the size of the cake tin, and place on top of the cake. Brush the marzipan with the beaten egg and brown under the grill (but be very careful not to let it burn). Decorate with a spray of silk flowers, and a band of ribbon round the cake.

To finish for Easter Brush the top of the cake with the warmed apricot jam. Roll out ¾ of the remaining marzipan to a round the size of the cake tin. Place on top of the cake. Brush the marzipan with the beaten egg. The remaining marzipan is shaped into 11 balls – to represent the Apostles, excluding Judas – and set round the edge of the cake. Brush with the beaten egg again and brown under the grill, again taking care not to let it burn. The centre of the cake can be decorated with small eggs and golden Easter chicks, and a band of ribbon placed round the cake.

PASSION SUNDAY

Passion Sunday is the fifth Sunday in Lent and marks the start of Passiontide when we particularly remember Christ's suffering on the cross. The word 'passion' comes from the Latin word 'passionem' meaning 'suffering'. In church, altars, statues and crosses are draped in purple, the colour of mourning.

This day is otherwise known as 'Carling Sunday', a derivation of the word 'care', which in Middle English means 'mourning'. 'Carling' is also the name of a type of grey parched pea which is popular in Scotland and the north of England and there seem to be a number of tales told about how these peas came to be the traditional Passion Sunday meal. The most likely is that its origin was the old pagan spring bean feast which was held at this time of year. In Northumberland the custom was to hide a pea in the dish at dinner and whoever got the pea would be the first to marry. There are many regional variations of the traditional dish of Carling Peas. The Northumberland tradition was to boil the soaked peas, then fry and butter them, finishing them off with a dash of rum.

It is generally thought that the real reason for eating carlings was poverty. Nearing the end of Lent, all the cheap, flavoursome food available would have been eaten, and the poor would not have been able to afford some of the alternatives available to supplement the meagre Lent meals. Carling peas would have been an important source of protein in their meat-less diet.

Passion Cake

From Elizabeth Jenkins, Castleton, Cardiff

This particular recipe has been thoroughly tried and tested many times.

Makes 2×8-in (20-cm) cakes

4 oz (100 g) self-raising flour
4 oz (100 g) wholemeal self-raising
* flour*
1 teaspoon baking powder
1 teaspoon cinnamon
3 oz (75 g) caster sugar
6 fl oz (175 ml) sunflower oil
4 eggs
6 oz (175 g) carrots, grated
2 oz (50 g) walnuts, chopped

For the topping
8 oz (225 g) low fat cream cheese
8 teaspoons lemon juice
2 oz (50 g) icing sugar
4 walnut halves, chopped

Pre-heat the oven to 375°F (190°C), gas mark 5.

Grease and line 2×8-in (20-cm) round tins. Sift the flours, baking powder and cinnamon into a large mixing bowl. Stir in the sugar. Mix the oil into the dry ingredients and beat in the eggs, one at a time. Mix well, and add the carrots and walnuts. Pour the batter into the cake tins and bake in a moderately hot oven for 40 minutes, or until firm. Allow to cool.

To make the topping, beat all the ingredients except the walnuts together until smooth. Sandwich the 2 cakes together with half the mixture and drizzle the rest over the top of the cake. Sprinkle with the chopped walnuts.

✿ GOOD FRIDAY ✿

'It was now about the sixth hour, and darkness came over the whole land until the ninth hour, for the sun stopped shining. And the curtain of the temple was torn in two. Jesus called out with a loud voice, "Father, into your hands I commit my spirit". When he had said this, he breathed his last.'
(Luke 23 : 44 – 46)

Good Friday is the Friday before Easter Day and it is the most solemn day in the Church Year, as we commemorate Christ's crucifixion on the cross. No church bells may toll, except for a funeral, and altars are left bare to symbolise mourning.

The main Good Friday service is from 12 noon onwards, consisting of prayer and meditation interspersed with readings, short sermons and hymns, like 'There Is a Green Hill Far Away'. The service commemorates the suffering of Jesus on the cross and ends at 3.00 p.m. (the ninth hour), the time of Jesus's death. A symbolic Good Friday ritual before the Reformation was to take from the church an image of Christ, a consecrated 'host' or a crucifix, and bury it in a sepulchre. This was then watched over until Easter Day when it was 'resurrected'.

Traditionally, Hot Cross Buns are eaten for breakfast on Good Friday and they are distinguished by the mark of the cross. It seems they originate from the pagan celebration of the spring equinox when similar buns were eaten and cut with a cross to help the dough rise, as was the case with all bread. However, following the Reformation, the new Protestant order denounced the crosses as superstitious, so they were only allowed for special holy cakes. At one time all the bread for Easter Day was baked on Good Friday as it was believed that this bread would protect all, including animals, from ills and evil. So a loaf would be baked dry and then hung up. If anyone was suffering from illness the dry loaf would be grated into their milk in the belief that it would cure them.

As Good Friday was once a day of general abstinence and fasting, fish is still the traditional meal. In some households it is still the custom to eat fish every Friday.

Hot Cross Buns

From Mrs Carol Porter, Wombourne, South Staffordshire

This is the start of my Easter cooking. They are made on Maundy Thursday so that we can have Hot Cross Buns for breakfast on Good Friday before going to the special children's service at church. In the original recipe, a shorter proving time was stated, but Maundy Thursday is a very busy day for me, so the longer time suits me very well.

Makes about 8 buns

1 pint (600 ml) milk
1½ oz (40 g) fresh yeast
2 lb (1 kg) wholemeal flour
2 teaspoons salt
2 teaspoons mixed spice
4 tablespoons honey

4 oz (100 g) butter
4 oz (100 g) currants, soaked in hot water until soft
6 tablespoons warmed honey to glaze

Warm half of the milk, mix with yeast, and leave for about 5 minutes. Mix the flours, salt and spice in a large warmed bowl. Heat the rest of the milk to boiling point and stir in the honey and butter. Allow to cool. Add to the flour with the drained currants and yeast mixture. Mix, then knead well (adding more milk or flour if necessary to make a smooth dough). Cover with plastic and a tea towel and leave in a cool place for 3 hours. Knock back, then leave to rise for a further 2 hours. Knock back again and cut into 4-oz (100-g) pieces, moulding into 'buns'. Put to prove again for 40 minutes. Pre-heat the oven to 400°F (200°C), gas mark 6. Cut a deep cross on each bun and prove again for 10 minutes. Bake for 25 minutes. Brush with warmed honey immediately afterwards to glaze.

Hint for Hot Cross Buns

From Mrs E. Jones, Burton Joyce, Nottingham

When rolling out your hot cross buns, make them oval instead of round so that you can mark them with a proper-shaped cross. This is the way we always made them in Yorkshire.

Baked Cod

From Mrs M. Crinson, Aylesham, Canterbury

This fish dish has been served on Good Fridays from one generation to the next in our family.

Serves 4 to 6

8 oz (225 g) breadcrumbs	*A little salt*
4 oz (100 g) shredded suet	*Chopped parsley*
Juice of 1 lemon	*2 lb (1 kg) of cod fillets*
1 or 2 eggs	*¼ pint (150 ml) white wine*

Pre-heat the oven to 375°F (190°C), gas mark 5.

Make the stuffing first by mixing together all the ingredients except for the cod and white wine. Wash and trim the cod. Place in a well-greased ovenproof dish, add the wine and arrange the stuffing round the fish. Cover with greaseproof paper, place in the oven and cook for 45 minutes. Remove the paper and brown for a few minutes before serving.

Lord Soper's Sole au Gratin

This recipe is actually a choice made by my wife, and for a good reason: I haven't a favourite dish but whenever she cooks this one it is a delight to eat it.

Serves 4

8 fillets of sole or plaice, skinned	*Juice of ½ lemon*
and rolled	*Juice of ½ orange*
½ pint (300 ml) milk	*¼ pint (150 ml) yoghurt*
1 oz (25 g) butter	*¼ pint (150 ml) soured cream*
1 oz (25 g) flour	*4 tablespoons brown breadcrumbs*
2 oz (50 g) Cheddar cheese, grated	

Place the fish in a saucepan with the milk and poach over a low heat for about 30 minutes until the fish flakes when tested with a fork. Drain the fish, and mix ½ pint (300 ml) of the liquid with the butter and flour. Place in a saucepan over a low heat, stirring continuously, until the sauce thickens. Cook for 2 minutes then mix in the grated cheese. Pre-heat the oven to 350°F (180°C), gas mark 4. Put the fish in a baking dish and squeeze over the lemon and orange juice. Cover the fish with the yoghurt and soured cream and pour the cheese sauce on top. Sprinkle freely with brown breadcrumbs. Put in the oven on the top shelf. When heated through, if not brown on the top, put under the grill for a few seconds.

Salmon Fish Pie

From Mrs Doreen M. Jones, Sutton, Surrey

This makes a lovely 'Friday Fish Day' recipe, or is especially tasty after the Good Friday Procession of Witness in our town!

Serves 4

4 oz (100 g) breadcrumbs
2 lb (1 kg) potatoes, peeled, boiled
and mashed with butter, pepper
and salt
1×7½-oz (210-g) tin of red salmon,
chopped
1×7-oz (200-g) tin of pilchards in
tomato, bones and skin removed,
and broken up into pieces

1 dessertspoon anchovy sauce
1 dessertspoon tomato sauce or
purée
2 teaspoons mixed herbs
2 teaspoons fresh parsley, chopped
Salt and pepper
1 egg (size 3), beaten
Butter for topping

Pre-heat the oven to 350°F (180°C), gas mark 4.
Grease a flameproof dish with butter and place a good sprinkling of breadcrumbs in the bottom. Put the mashed potato into a large bowl and make a well in the middle. Add the salmon and pilchards, and fold in thoroughly, being careful not to break up the fish meat too much. Add the anchovy sauce, tomato sauce or purée, herbs, parsley, and salt and pepper to taste, and again fold in. Gently mix in the egg. Fork the whole mixture into the prepared dish and cover fairly thickly with the remaining breadcrumbs. Dot the top generously with butter. Cook for approximately 45 minutes.

The mixture is delicious eaten hot or cold with salad. It can also be made into fish cakes, when coated in egg and breadcrumbs and fried in cooking oil, then drained on kitchen paper.

Prawn Cocktail Sauce

From Mrs Doreen M. Jones, Sutton, Surrey

This is a tasty sauce for any fish dish.

Makes about 4 fl oz (100 ml)

1 heaped tablespoon 'Marvel'
3 dessertspoons water (approx)
1 tablespoon salad cream
2 tablespoons tomato ketchup

½ teaspoon Worcestershire sauce
3 teaspoons horseradish sauce
Salt and pepper to taste

Mix the 'Marvel' to liquid with the water. Add the salad cream, tomato ketchup, Worcestershire sauce and horseradish sauce. Mix this all together well. Add salt and pepper to taste. If a thinner consistency is required, add approximately 1 tablespoon of vinegar.

Fillets of St Peter's Fish

From Mrs Nina Ball, Cricklewood, London

This recipe was brought back from Israel.

Serves 6

2 tablespoons butter
1 medium onion, chopped
Salt and white pepper
Worcestershire sauce
Juice of 1 lemon

6 St Peter's fish fillets
9 fresh mushrooms, sliced
3 tablespoons fresh dill, chopped
6 fl oz (175 ml) dry white wine
Hollandaise sauce to serve

Pre-heat the oven to 375°F (190°C), gas mark 5.

Grease a baking dish with 1 tablespoon of butter. Sprinkle on half of the chopped onion, salt, pepper, a dash of Worcestershire sauce and half of the lemon juice. Place the fillets in the dish. Sprinkle with the remaining chopped onion, sliced mushrooms, chopped dill, salt, pepper, a dash of Worcestershire sauce and the remaining lemon juice and wine. Dot the fillets with the remaining butter. Cover the baking dish with foil and bake for about 8 to 10 minutes. Serve with Hollandaise sauce.

Ackee and Saltfish

From Bobbette McFarlane, Researcher, Good Morning Sunday

This is the national dish of Jamaica. It is a great favourite eaten either as a main meal or as a breakfast dish before going to church on Sundays and Good Friday.

Serves 4

1 lb (450 g) saltfish (cod)
4 oz (100 g) margarine
2 rashers of bacon, derinded and
* chopped*
2 medium tomatoes, chopped

1 medium chilli or sweet pepper,
* chopped (optional)*
A pinch of thyme
Salt and black pepper
1 × 15-oz (425-g) tin ackee, drained

Boil the fish in water for 10 minutes or soak overnight. Wash the fish to remove any excess salt. Remove the skin and bones and flake the fish. Melt the margarine in a saucepan and gently fry the bacon for 3 minutes. Add the tomatoes, chilli or pepper and thyme and cook for a further 5 minutes, stirring gently. Add the fish, and season with salt and black pepper to taste. Cook for 10 minutes. Add the ackee and cook for 8 to 10 minutes, stirring gently.

This dish is usually served with potatoes, yams or plantain. Ackee is available from many branches of Tesco's, large stores with an 'ethnic' section, West Indian and Asian shops.

Max Bygraves'
Fresh Trout en Papillote

Serves 4

4 trout
4 oz (100 g) butter, softened

2 oz (50 g) chives or parsley or
* mixed herbs, finely chopped*

Clean and gut the fish. Blend the herbs of your choice into the butter and use to stuff the trout. Wrap the trout neatly in greased foil, then place under a hot grill or on a barbecue for 4 to 5 minutes, until the fish is cooked through. Allow the diners to open the foil parcels themselves to get the full benefit of the aroma. These are excellent served with a tomato and onion salad, plus a glass of Chablis – delicious!

❦ EASTER ❦

'The angel said to the women, "Do not be afraid, for I know that you are looking for Jesus, who was crucified. He is not here; he has risen, just as he said."'
(Matthew 28 : 5 & 6)

Easter is the most important of all the Christian festivals, when we celebrate the Resurrection of Jesus Christ, symbolising the defeat of death and sin, and the victory of light over darkness. Easter is always a Sunday, but it is a movable feast that can fall any time between 21 March and 25 April. In the Western Church it is calculated as the first Sunday after the full moon of spring on or after 21 March, but if the first full moon falls on a Sunday, Easter Day is a week later.

It is thought that the name Easter could derive from Eostre, the name of the pagan Saxon spring goddess. Easter is a great time of rejoicing for Christians who attend church and take communion. Churches are decorated with spring flowers and the church bells ring out. Traditionally, the congregation wear a new piece of clothing or a new 'Easter' bonnet – which stems from the idea that those who were being baptised at Easter, as was the custom, should wear new white garments. It was usual to show off the new outfit by parading around the town, thus the Easter parade came about.

The most familiar Easter symbols are the egg and the rabbit. The egg was originally a pagan symbol of rebirth, but before the Reformation it became customary on Easter Day to take eggs that were forbidden during Lent into church to be blessed. The egg has since been seen to symbolise the resurrection in that beyond the hard, lifeless shell is new life ready to be born. Hard-boiled, dyed eggs were used in Easter games all over Britain – Pace Egg-rolling was one of the favourites, especially in northern England – which accounts for the nickname, 'Pace Egg Day'.

The rabbit, or Easter bunny, is extremely fertile and was thus a pagan symbol of the coming of new life at spring time. Although today's Easter bunny appears in chocolate and on greeting cards, it seems there is no specific Christian interpretation.

One of the main symbols of Easter is the paschal lamb, referring to the lamb slaughtered at the Jewish Passover and to Christ, the Lamb of God. The main meal of Easter, by tradition, has to be roast lamb!

Easter Bread ○

From Mrs B. Armstrong, Manchester

Makes 1 × 2-lb (1-kg) loaf

8 oz (225 g) plain flour
2 teaspoons baking powder
¼ teaspoon mixed spice
½ teaspoon cinnamon
3 oz (75 g) butter or lard

3 oz (75 g) sugar
2 oz (50 g) dates, chopped
2 oz (50 g) sultanas
1 egg, well beaten

Pre-heat the oven to 375°F (190°C), gas mark 5.
Sieve the flour, baking powder, mixed spice and cinnamon into a bowl. Rub in the butter or lard until the mixture resembles fine breadcrumbs. Add the sugar, dates and sultanas. Mix together well, adding the egg. Put the mixture in a greased 2-lb (1-kg) loaf tin and bake at the bottom of the oven for 30 minutes, then reduce the heat to 350°F (180°C), gas mark 4 and bake for a further 30 minutes.

Easter Lamb ○

From Mrs Jackie Baber, St Peter Port, Guernsey

Serves 6 to 8

4–5 sprigs fresh mint
1 sprig of fresh rosemary or 1
  teaspoon dried rosemary
4 tablespoons olive oil
1 leg lamb

3–4 rashers bacon
1 clove garlic, finely chopped
1 tablespoon parsley, finely
  chopped

Pre-heat the oven to 350°F (180°C), gas mark 4.
Place the washed sprigs of mint and the fresh rosemary, if used, in the bottom of a meat dish with the olive oil. Place the meat on top, lay the strips of bacon over the lamb and sprinkle with a mixture of finely chopped garlic and parsley, plus the dried rosemary, if the fresh has not been used. Cook in a moderate oven, allowing 25 to 30 minutes per 1 lb (450 g) cooking time. Baste the joint from time to time as necessary. Remove the bacon and serve.

Large, lean gigot chops may be cooked in the same way for about 30 to 45 minutes.

Traditional West Country Easter Biscuits

From Mrs Ada E. Hammond, Haslemere, Surrey

I was born and brought up in Somerset and these biscuits were a firm favourite of mine when I was a child. Now, seventy plus years later, I still find them delicious. The secret is not to overdo the oil of cassia – I find about 3 drops is sufficient for this quantity.

Makes about 15 biscuits

2 oz (50 g) margarine	*½ oz (15 g) currants*
1½ oz (40 g) caster sugar	*3 oz (75 g) plain flour*
1 egg yolk or ½ egg	*Egg white, lightly beaten*
3 drops of oil of cassia	*Caster sugar for dusting*

Pre-heat the oven to 325°F (160°C), gas mark 3.

Cream the margarine and sugar. Add the egg or egg yolk. Cream again, then add the oil of cassia, the currants and the flour. Knead, then roll out thinly and cut into 2-in (5-cm) rounds with a fluted pastry cutter. Place the biscuits on a greased baking sheet and bake in a moderate oven for about 10 minutes. Remove from the oven, brush with egg white and dust with caster sugar, then return the biscuits to the oven for a further 5 minutes. The biscuits should be light in colour; overcooking will spoil them.

Serve the biscuits stacked and tied with a ribbon.

Easter Nests

From Mrs C. Storey, Frinton-on-Sea, Essex

This is a recipe which appeals to children, they can make it and eat it! We use it in our playgroup at Easter time and it gives us a good opportunity to explain about the Easter message of new life.

Makes about 10 nests

2 oz (50 g) cocoa	*6 oz (175 g) shredded wheat,*
6 oz (175 g) margarine	*crushed*
4 oz (100 g) soft dark brown sugar	*Icing sugar*
4 oz (100 g) golden syrup	*Egg white*
	Food colouring

Melt the cocoa, margarine, sugar and syrup in a saucepan over a low heat until they are quite hot, but not boiling. Remove from the heat and mix in the crushed shredded wheat. Shape into 10 nest shapes, place on a greased baking tray and leave to cool and set.

The eggs can be made out of icing sugar folded into whisked egg white, and coloured with food colouring.

Mrs Marilyn Butcher of Chorleywood, Hertfordshire, suggests filling the Easter Nests with chocolate mini eggs.

Lemon Paradise ○

From Mrs Joan Nuttall, Bacup, Lancashire

Lemon Paradise is our special treat on Easter Day. It reminds us that Jesus is now in paradise after his suffering on the cross.

Serves 4

1×11-oz (300-g) can condensed
  milk (sweetened)
Grated rind and juice of 2 lemons
3 large eggs, separated
1 packet trifle sponges

For decoration
  ¼ pint (150 ml) whipping cream
  3 lemon slices, cut into quarters

Lightly grease a 2-lb (1-kg) loaf tin and line with cling film. Pour the condensed milk into a bowl, stir in the lemon rind and juice with the egg yolks. Whisk the egg whites until they are stiff and stand in peaks. Using a metal spoon, fold the egg whites into the thickening lemon mixture. Cut the sponges into 4 pieces. Place pieces of sponge in the base of the tin. Spoon in one-third of the lemon filling and continue to layer the 2 ingredients, ending with a layer of sponge. Cover the surface with more cling film and leave in a cool place for at least 24 hours, so that the sponge and lemon filling merge together.

To serve, whip the cream until it holds its shape. Put half in a piping bag. Carefully turn the loaf on to a serving plate and pipe rows of stars on the top. Place the lemon pieces on top. Serve in slices with the remaining cream.

Apricot Brandy Cheesecake

From Mrs Gwen Aird, Willowbank, Wick, Caithness

This is delicious and the apricots on top of the cheesecake remind me of Easter eggs. I feel after giving up all candy and sweets for Lent, one could splurge and have a special dessert. This is a Canadian recipe and I make it for special occasions.

Serves 10

8 oz (225 g) digestive biscuit crumbs
2 tablespoons sugar
1½ oz (40 g) butter or margarine,
  melted
For the filling
  1 oz (25 g) unflavoured gelatine
  8 oz (225 g) white sugar
  8 fl oz (250 ml) apricot syrup (from
    tin of apricot halves)
  4 oz (100 g) apricot brandy
  2 oz (50 g) lemon juice
  4 egg yolks

2 × 9-oz (250-g) packs of
  Philadelphia cream cheese,
  softened
4 egg whites
8 oz (225 g) whipping cream,
  whipped
For the topping
  2 × 14-oz (400-g) cans apricot halves
    in light syrup, drained
  4 oz (100 g) apricot brandy
  2 tablespoons cornflour

Pre-heat the oven to 325°F (160°C), gas mark 3.

Mix together the biscuit crumbs, 2 tablespoons of sugar and the melted butter or margarine. Press into the bottom of a 9-in (23-cm) spring form cake tin. Bake in the oven for 10 minutes.

To make the filling, put the gelatine, half of the white sugar, the apricot syrup, 4 oz (100 g) apricot brandy and the lemon juice into a medium-sized saucepan. Whisk in the egg yolks. Cook over a medium heat for 8 to 10 minutes, stirring constantly, until the mixture has thickened. Remove from the heat. Beat the cream cheese in a large bowl until smooth. Gradually pour in the gelatine mixture. Chill until slightly thickened. Beat the egg white until it stands in soft peaks, then gradually beat in the remaining 4 oz (100 g) sugar, beating until it stands in stiff peaks. Fold into the thickened gelatine mixture, along with the whipped cream. Turn into the crumb-lined cake tin. Smooth the top. Chill for several hours or until firm.

To make the topping, cover the top of the cheesecake with apricot halves. In a small saucepan combine the apricot brandy and the cornflour. Cook and stir over a medium heat until the mixture is thickened and clear. Allow to cool slightly before brushing or spooning over the top of the cheesecake.

Easter Bonnet Cake

From Mrs Eileen Jackson, Aston, Sheffield

This is baked in the shape of an Easter bonnet. It is a 'healthy' cake and a great favourite in our family.

Makes 1 × 8-in (20-cm) cake

3 eggs
3 oz (75 g) muscovado sugar
3 oz (75 g) wholemeal self-raising
flour
1 oz (25 g) carob powder
1 tablespoon warm water

For the filling
3 oz (75 g) icing sugar
1½ oz (40 g) polyunsaturated
margarine
For the icing
4½ oz (120 g) bars carob
1 oz (25 g) polyunsaturated
margarine

Pre-heat the oven to 400°F (200°C), gas mark 6.

Grease and line a 6-in (15-cm) sandwich tin and an 8-in (20-cm) sandwich tin to form the bonnet's brim. Break the eggs into a mixing bowl, add the sugar and whisk over hot water until the mixture is thick and creamy. Leave to stand for a few minutes. Remove the bowl from the heat and whisk until the mixture is cool and leaves a trail when the whisk is lifted out of the mixture. Carefully fold in the flour and carob powder using a metal spoon. Stir in the water. Divide the mixture between the 2 tins. Bake in the oven for 12 to 25 minutes or until the cakes are firm to the touch. Remove from the tins and allow to cool before filling and icing.

Meanwhile, make the filling by creaming the margarine and icing sugar together. Place half of the filling in a piping bag. When the cakes are cold, spread the filling on the underside of the smaller cake and place it on top of the larger cake to form the bonnet shape.

For the icing, melt the carob and margarine in a bowl over a pan of hot water. When they are melted, cover the bonnet completely with the icing using a metal knife to create a smooth surface. When the icing is set, pipe the remaining filling mixture round the brim of the bonnet. If liked, pin on a small curled ribbon or a flower.

❧ ROGATION SUNDAY ❧

Rogation Sunday is the fifth Sunday after Easter. The period we call 'Rogationtide' includes this day and the three following which lead up to Ascension Day on the Thursday. (Ascension Day is forty days after Easter and commemorates Christ's Ascension into Heaven.) At one time abstinence and penitence were the hallmarks of Rogationtide, when God's protection and blessing was sought on the crops.

The ancient custom practised on this day was 'Beating the Bounds', when the parish clergy would lead the parishioners around the village boundary. Most were illiterate and maps were not widely available, so this practice ensured that all knew where the boundary lay. Stone boundary markers were left at key points and the village boys would beat these with staves. The priest would lead the singing of psalms, read the Rogationtide Gospel and recite passages of Scripture,

'Cursed be he that removeth his neighbour's landmark.'
(Deuteronomy 27 : 17)

Rogation Sunday Vegetarian Oat and Onion Roast

From Kerena Marchant, Researcher, Songs of Praise

I became vegetarian out of a desire to preserve life and the Creator's creation. Rogation Sunday is a Christian interpretation of the pagan festival of Beltaine – which was a Festival of Life. On Rogation Sunday I reflect on the harvests to come during the year throughout the world (varied as they may be) and the precious gift of life that I share with all creation.

Serves 4

2 large onions, finely chopped
2 oz (50 g) margarine
1 free-range egg, beaten
3 oz (75 g) rolled oats
4–6 oz (100–175 g) vegetarian
* Cheddar cheese (or ordinary*
* Cheddar cheese), grated*

1 teaspoon yeast extract
1 teaspoon mixed herbs
Salt and pepper to taste
1 tomato to garnish

Pre-heat the oven to 375°F (190°C), gas mark 5.
Fry the onions in the margarine until they are transparent. Beat the egg (if
you want a lighter bake, just beat the egg-white) until it is stiff. Transfer the
cooked onions to a mixing bowl and add the oats, cheese, yeast extract,
herbs and seasoning. Mix the ingredients together. Finally add the beaten
egg and mix with the other ingredients. Transfer the mixture to a greased
10×8×2-in (25×20×5-cm) ovenproof baking dish. Slice the tomato and
decorate the bake with the slices. Bake for 30 to 40 minutes until brown.
Serve with traditional Sunday vegetables and give the gravy boat a holiday!

❦ SPRING SUNDAY LUNCHES ❦

Kathy Staff's Soured Cream Pork Chops

This dish is ideal for a very quick meal, besides being tasty and looking good.

Serves 2

2 pork chops (chump not loin)	1×5-oz (150-g) carton soured cream
Salt and pepper	A pinch of paprika

Pre-heat the oven to 400°F (200°C), gas mark 6.
Seal the pork chops in a frying pan by briefly frying in a little fat or butter.
When sealed, transfer to a small baking tin, season well, pour over the
carton of soured cream and sprinkle with paprika. Bake for 20 minutes,
depending on the size of chops. Serve with jacket potatoes.

Dame Vera Lynn's Turkey Escalopes

This is my favourite recipe because I get great enjoyment preparing and eating it.

Serves 2

1 large onion	1×6-oz (175-g) tin tomatoes or 3–4
1 clove garlic, crushed	fresh tomatoes
Butter and oil	A pinch of basil or oregano
	2 escalopes of turkey breast

Sauté the onion and garlic in a little butter and oil. Add the tomatoes and
basil or oregano. Cover and simmer for about 30 minutes. Then sauté the
escalopes of turkey breast in butter with some garlic, if liked. When nearly
cooked, pour the sauce over and simmer for a little while before serving.
Serve with buttered noodles, rice or peas, and a green salad.

Mary Archer's Mince Duxelles

Rich, delicious, filling – and economical!

Serves 4

2 oz (50 g) butter
2 small onions, chopped
8 oz (225 g) mushrooms, chopped
1 tablespoon thyme, finely chopped
1 tablespoon parsley, finely
  chopped

3 tablespoons white breadcrumbs
Salt and pepper
1 egg
1 lb (450 g) minced beef
4 oz (100 g) mature Cheddar cheese,
  grated

Pre-heat the oven to 375°F (190°C), gas mark 5.

To make the stuffing, melt 1 oz (25 g) butter in a frying pan, and fry the onions gently for a few minutes. Then add mushrooms, thyme and parsley. Cook briskly for 5 minutes, then remove from the heat and add the breadcrumbs and seasoning. Leave to cool slightly. Beat the egg and add to the mince with a little seasoning to taste. Divide the mince into 8 portions and flatten each portion into an oblong shape. Place 1 tablespoon of cooled stuffing on the shaped mince, and roll it up into a sausage. Place in a greased ovenproof dish and bake in a moderately hot oven for about 30 minutes. Meanwhile, mix the grated cheese with 1 oz (25 g) butter. Remove the duxelles from the oven and spread with the cheese and butter mixture. Replace in the oven for a further 10 minutes, or until the top is crisply browned.

Serve with creamed potatoes and a selection of vegetables and gravy.

Liver à la Christie

From Mr Michael Christie, Ludgershall, Buckinghamshire

Serves 4

1 oz (25 g) butter
2 medium sized onions, finely
  sliced
1 large clove garlic, crushed
½ teaspoon mixed herbs or tarragon

8 slices liver, about ½-in (1-cm)
  thick
1 teaspoon French mustard
1 wine glass red wine
Salt and black pepper

Melt the butter in a large frying pan, and fry the onions gently until soft. Add the crushed garlic and herbs. Mix together and draw to one side of the pan. Place the liver in the pan and fry for 2 minutes on one side, then turn and fry for 1 minute on the other side. Cut each piece of liver across into strips about ¾-in (2-cm) wide while it is still cooking. This should only take about 1 minute so the liver will have cooked for a total of 4 minutes. Mix the mustard into the wine, and add to the pan. Mix all the ingredients together, season to taste, and cook for another 3 minutes at a high heat.

An alternative is to flame with brandy at this point and cook for 1 minute, then add 3 to 4 tablespoons of double cream.

Serve on a bed of savoury rice or with vegetables of your choice.

Sigh of a Nun or 'Suspiros De Monja'

From Mr Neville Measures, Dartmouth, Devon

I spend quite a few months in the year working as a travel guide in Spain and have come across this recipe.

Serves 6

8 fl oz (250 ml) milk	*3 oz (75 g) sugar*
Grated rind of 1 lemon	*8 oz (225 g) flour*
2 tablespoons butter	*6 eggs*
A pinch of salt	*Oil for frying*

Heat the milk with the lemon rind, butter, salt and sugar. When it begins to boil, stir in the sifted flour until it becomes a thick paste. Allow to cool a little. Add the eggs one by one, stirring well after each addition. Heat the oil in a saucepan or a deep frying pan. Reduce the heat a little, and put in walnut-sized spoonsful of the paste. They will fry themselves, so there is no need to touch them. They will open, turn over and puff up. Serve hot and well-drained, sprinkled with sugar or hot syrup.

Hilary's Quick Chocolate Mousse ○

From Hilary Mayo, Producer, Good Morning Sunday

Chocolate is my weakness, so this is one of my favourite desserts. I find it ideal when we have friends for Sunday lunch. When I have been up early to produce *Good Morning Sunday* and then go off to church, I do not have a great deal of time, so this I can prepare the night before, or very quickly before church.

Serves 2

2 oz (50 g) plain chocolate   *Double cream, whipped*
2 eggs, separated   *Grated chocolate to decorate*

Melt the chocolate in a bowl over hot, but not boiling, water. Beat the egg yolks, then stir them into the melted chocolate. Beat the whites until stiff and fold them into the mixture. Pour into individual dishes and leave to set. Decorate with the cream and chocolate.

For a richer recipe on special occasions: double the quantity of chocolate, then when you are ready to serve, make a few small holes in the top of each mousse and spoon some rum or brandy over the surface. When the alcohol has soaked in, top with whipped cream and grated chocolate.

Grand Marnier Mousse ○

From Mrs June Caton, Tadley, Hampshire

Serves 6 to 8

4 large eggs, separated   *12 fl oz (350 ml) whipping cream*
100 g (4 oz) sugar   *5 tablespoons Grand Marnier*
¾ oz (20 g) unflavoured gelatine   *16 lady or boudoir finger biscuits*
5 tablespoons cold water   *(optional)*

Beat the egg yolks with the sugar until very thick and creamy. In a small pan sprinkle the gelatine on to the water and leave to soak for approximately 5 minutes. Heat over a low heat to dissolve the gelatine. Whip the cream lightly. Beat the egg whites until they stand in soft peaks. Combine the egg yolks and sugar with the cream, add the gelatine and Grand Marnier. Fold in the egg whites. Line a 2-pint (1.2-l) mould or soufflé dish with the boudoir biscuits, if using. Turn the mousse into the mould and allow to set for 4 hours.

3
Summer

✤ WHITSUN ✤

'When the day of Pentecost came, they were all together in one place.
Suddenly a sound like the blowing of a violent wind came from
heaven and filled the whole house where they were sitting. They saw
what seemed to be tongues of fire that separated and came to rest on
each of them. All of them were filled with the Holy Spirit and began
to speak in other tongues as the Spirit enabled them.'
(Acts 2 : 1 – 4)

Whit Sunday is the time we celebrate the Feast of Pentecost, fifty days after Easter, when the Apostles were filled with the Holy Spirit. This marks the beginning of the Christian Church. The origin of the name 'Whitsun' is 'White Sunday', which refers to the customary white garments worn by those who were baptised on this day.

Pentecost is a joyous occasion, and is the second festival of the Church, after Easter. The churches are decked with flowers, the altar is draped in red (the liturgical colour) and traditional hymns, like 'Come, Holy Ghost', are sung.

There are many customs associated with Whitsun, but the best known must be the 'Whitwalks' whereby, traditionally, churches hold processions through the streets as an act of witness. Another feature in many parishes was 'Whitsun Ales', supposedly to raise money for the parish funds. Ale was brewed and the girls of the parish would exchange it for money. A Lord and Lady of the Ale ruled the day. Sometimes Whitcakes were also sold to raise money. Whitcakes and gooseberry pies have always been a feature of Whitsun, the latter no doubt deriving from the tradition that cooks would try to serve the 'first fruits' of the season on a special occasion.

Whitsuntide Cake

From Mrs G. S. Moynihan, Alton, Hampshire

These cakes were traditionally eaten in the north of Lincolnshire and possibly in other areas also. This particular recipe comes from Kirton in Lincolnshire and is dated 1890.

The cakes should be kept for some days in an air-tight container before being used as the flavour improves as the cakes mature. They are still fresh at the end of a fortnight.

Makes 2×8-in (20-cm) cakes

12 oz (350 g) butter
A pinch of salt
1½ lb (750 g) flour
½ pint (300 ml) milk
1 oz (25 g) yeast

For the filling
1 lb (450 g) currants
1 lb (450 g) moist brown sugar
2 oz (50 g) butter
½ teaspoon nutmeg
½ teaspoon allspice
1 egg yolk
2 tablespoons water
Egg white to glaze

Rub half the butter and the salt into the flour. Warm the remaining butter with the milk. Mix the yeast with a little lukewarm water, and then add it to the milk and butter mixture. Pour this mixture into the flour and knead it into a soft dough. Cover and leave in a warm place to rise. Place all the ingredients for the filling into a saucepan and warm them over a low heat until the currants are soft, so they will be quite done when the cake is baked.

When the dough is light and slightly risen, roll out one-quarter of the dough into an 8-in (20-cm) circle. Pre-heat the oven to 375°F (190°C), gas mark 5. Cover with one-third of the filling. Repeat this till there are 4 layers of dough and 3 of currant mixture. Fasten the edges well together with the white of the egg, taking care that no air is shut into the cake. Bake in a moderately hot oven for 30 minutes. Remove from the oven and brush over the top of the cake with egg white. Return to the oven for a further 30 to 45 minutes.

Gooseberry Lattice Tart ○

From Mrs B. Armstrong, Manchester

Serves 4

1 lb (450 g) hard green cooking
gooseberries, topped and tailed
1 tablespoon lemon juice
4 oz (100 g) soft brown sugar

2 oz (50 g) granulated sugar
2 tablespoons cornflour
6 oz (175 g) shortcrust pastry

Pre-heat the oven to 425°F (220°C), gas mark 7.

Place the gooseberries in a saucepan with the lemon juice and a little water and gently simmer them until tender. Stir in the brown sugar. Mix the granulated sugar and cornflour together and add sufficient water to make a paste. Add to the fruit and bring to the boil, stirring well all the time. Then simmer until the mixture thickens. Allow to cool.

Use most of the pastry to line a greased deep pie plate. Transfer the fruit mixture to the pastry case. Use the pastry trimmings, rolled and cut into narrow strips, to make a lattice design on top of the tart. Bake in the oven for about 25 minutes or until cooked through.

You can serve this delicious pudding hot or cold with whipped cream or custard.

❀ TRINITY SUNDAY ❀

Trinity Sunday falls on the Sunday after Whitsuntide and it honours the three persons of the Trinity – God the Father, God the Son, and God the Holy Spirit – but these three persons are believed to be as one and inseparable.

Many find this difficult to understand and in fact when the Roman Catholic Church separated from the Orthodox Church in the eleventh century it was the result of a disagreement about the Holy Trinity. The feast of the Holy Trinity was not officially recognised until 1334, but since then many churches have been dedicated to the Holy Trinity.

Coventry Godcakes

From Sue Goodman, Castle Bromwich, Birmingham

During the sixteenth century it was the custom in Coventry for godparents to give their godchildren cakes for good luck at the time of their confirmation. The cakes were usually triangular turnovers whose three points were said to represent the Holy Trinity (so they are equally suitable for Trinity Sunday). The size of the cake denoted the wealth of the giver, and each family tried to outdo the others.

Makes 12 turnovers

12 oz (350 g) puff or flaky pastry   1 beaten egg, to seal and glaze
8 oz (225 g) mincemeat or jam   Granulated sugar

Pre-heat the oven to 425°F (220°C), gas mark 7.
Cut the pastry in half. Roll out each piece on a lightly floured board and trim to a rectangle about 12×8-in (30×20-cm). Cut each rectangle into 6×4-in (15×10-cm) squares and cut each square diagonally to give 2 triangles. There will be 24 triangles in all. Wet 2 baking sheets and arrange 6 triangles on each. Put a teaspoon of mincemeat or jam on the centre of these triangles. Brush the pastry edges lightly with beaten egg and cover with the remaining triangles. Press the edges together to seal. Brush the lids with beaten egg and make 3 slits in each with a sharp knife. Dredge each turnover liberally with granulated sugar. Bake in the centre of the pre-heated oven for 12 to 15 minutes until golden brown.
Serve these tasty turnovers warm with cream.

Three Bean Loaf or Trinity Sunday Special

From Nan Alexander, Battle, Sussex

This recipe comes from the Cayman Islands. There are three islands there, and there can't be three better beans than the Holy Trinity. It can be served to both vegetarians and non-vegetarians. It also causes a lot of interest whilst eating as those who are doing so, try and decide what meat it is made from.

Serves 6

1×15½-oz (440-g) tin chick peas, drained
1×15½-oz (440-g) tin red kidney beans, drained
8 oz (225 g) (prepared weight) fresh green beans, cooked and chopped (frozen will do, but are not as good)
4 oz (100 g) fresh mushrooms, chopped
4 oz (100 g) celery, chopped
1 medium-sized onion, chopped

1 tablespoon soy sauce
2 oz (50 g) walnuts, very finely chopped
2 teaspoons paprika
A dash of salt (preferably sea salt)
1 egg, beaten
1 tablespoon sunflower or corn oil
3 tablespoons flour
1×8-oz (225-g) tin tomato sauce (one with 'bits in' is best)

Pre-heat the oven to 375°F (190°C), gas mark 5.

Combine the chick peas and kidney beans in a large bowl. Mash with a potato masher. Add the green beans, mushrooms, celery, onion, soy sauce, walnuts, paprika, salt, egg, oil, flour and 3 tablespoons of the tomato sauce. Stir well to blend. Spoon the mixture into a 2-lb (1-kg) loaf tin. Bake in a moderately hot oven for 50 minutes. While the loaf is cooling slightly in the tin heat the remaining tomato sauce in a saucepan. Turn out the loaf, slice and serve with the sauce.

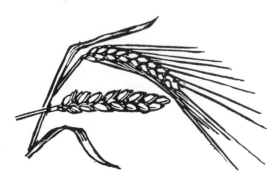

❦ CHURCH FÊTES AND TEAS ❦

Summer is the season of the church fête or tea. These are usually fund-raising events for charity or the church funds and at the same time are a good way of introducing members of the local community to the church. The fund-raising is usually done by selling items like books, plants and cakes; and the white elephant stall is always a great favourite. A tombola stall and games for children are usual activities as is the selling of afternoon teas to refresh the visitors.

These recipes should give you some interesting ideas for the cake stall and afternoon teas.

Bible Cake

From Miss June Houlmann, Formby, Merseyside

This used to be especially popular for chapel outings and teas, and is a good test of Bible knowledge.

Makes 1×8-in (20-cm) cake

(1) 8 oz (225 g) Judges V, v 25 (last clause)

(2) 8 oz (225 g) Jeremiah VI, v 20

(3) 1 tablespoon 1 Samuel XIV, v 25

(4) 3 Jeremiah XVII, v 11

(5) 8 oz (225 g) 1 Samuel XXX, v 12

(6) 8 oz (225 g) Nahum III, v 12, chopped

(7) 2 oz (50 g) Numbers XVII, v 8, blanched and chopped

(8) 1 lb (450 g) 1 Kings IV, v 22

(9) Season to taste with II Chronicles IX, v 9

(10) A pinch Leviticus II, v 13

(11) 1 teaspoon Amos IV, v 5

(12) 3 tablespoons Judges IV, v 19

Pre-heat the oven to 350°F (180°C), gas mark 4.

Beat numbers 1, 2 and 3 to a cream, add 4, one at a time, still beating; then add 5, 6 and 7 and beat again. Mix 8, 9, 10 and 11 together, then add to the mixture, then add number 12. If you have followed Solomon's advice (Proverbs XXIII v 14), then your cake will be good. Bake it in a moderate oven for 1½ hours.

Explanation

1 Butter; 2 Sugar; 3 Honey; 4 Eggs; 5 Raisins; 6 Figs (chopped); 7 Almonds (blanched and chopped); 8 Flour; 9 Spice (ground); 10 Salt; 11 Leaven (baking powder); 12 Milk.

And the advice of Solomon is to beat it well!

Vicarage Pâté ○

From Mrs Sue Harrison, Watton, Thetford, Norfolk

We call it Vicarage Pâté because it is cheap but good!

Serves 4

1 bay leaf
12 oz (350 g) streaky bacon,
derinded and stretched
12 oz (350 g) pig's liver, sinews
removed
4 oz (100 g) pork fat
1 small onion, quartered or chopped
1 clove garlic
1 teaspoon dried mixed herbs or 1
tablespoon fresh mixed herbs
(preferably parsley, thyme,
summer savoury and sage)

1 tablespoon fresh breadcrumbs or
1 round of bread (depending on
whether using a food processor or
mincer)
1 egg, beaten
1 tablespoon brandy or sherry
(optional)
Salt and pepper
1 oz (25 g) butter
1 oz (25 g) plain flour
½ pint (300 ml) milk
Butter to seal

Pre-heat the oven to 350°F (180°C), gas mark 4.

Grease a 2-lb (1-kg) loaf tin or oval ovenproof dish with butter. Place a bay leaf on the bottom centre of the dish. Line the bottom and sides of the dish with streaky bacon, overlapping the rashers.

If you are using a food processor with a metal blade, place the liver, pork fat, quarters of onion, garlic, herbs, 1 round of bread, egg and brandy or sherry into the processor. Process for 1 minute for coarse pâté, or a little longer for a finer pâté. Season well.

Make a thick white sauce by whisking together the butter, flour and milk over a low heat until the sauce thickens. Cook for a further minute, then add to the other ingredients.

If you are using a mincer, mince the liver and pork fat with the chopped onion, crushed garlic and chopped herbs. Mince a little longer for finer pâté. Add the breadcrumbs, egg, brandy or sherry, and seasoning and white sauce.

Pour the mixture into the prepared dish. Place in a baking tray of water so the water comes about 1 in (2.5 cm) up the sides of the loaf tin. Cook for approximately 30 minutes until the pâté is firm to the touch, slightly brown on top and coming away from the sides of the dish. Remove from the oven and coat with butter to seal. Allow to cool.

Either turn out on to a serving dish and decorate with slices of glacé cherry either side of the bay leaf, or wrap and place in the freezer where it will keep very well for 3 months. Alternatively, divide into 4 pieces, placing kitchen foil between each section. Wrap the whole pâté in kitchen foil and freeze. This makes it very easy to use a portion at a time.

General Eva Burrows'
Australian Fruit Cake

As World Leader of The Salvation Army, I'm very much an international person, but my roots and my heart are in Australia, where I was born – so I have chosen this Australian recipe. Knowing what busy lives people live today, this quick and easy recipe – suitable for any time of the year – might be particularly appreciated.

Makes 1×2-lb (1-kg) cake

4 oz (100 g) margarine
8 oz (225 g) sugar
8 fl oz (250 ml) water
12 oz (350 g) mixed dried fruit
(sultanas, raisins, cherries)
1 teaspoon bicarbonate of soda

2 teaspoons mixed spice
1 teaspoon ground ginger
4 oz (100 g) self-raising flour
4 oz (100 g) plain flour
1 egg, beaten

Pre-heat the oven to 325°F (160°C), gas mark 3.
Boil all the ingredients, except for the flour and egg, in a saucepan. When the mixture is cool, add the flour and beaten egg. Place the mixture in a greased 2-lb (1-kg) loaf tin and bake for 1 hour on the top shelf of the oven.

Carmen Silvera's
Walnut and Date Bread

It is a recipe which my step-mother gave me – I used to love her walnut and date bread – and I have found it easy to make and oh, so delicious!

Makes 1×2-lb (1-kg) loaf

8 oz (225 g) walnuts, chopped
1 lb (450 g) dates, chopped
16 fl oz (475 ml) boiling water
1 teaspoon bicarbonate of soda

3 oz (75 g) margarine
8 oz (225 g) self-raising flour
8 oz (225 g) sugar
1 egg, lightly beaten

Pre-heat the oven to 350°F (180°C), gas mark 4.
Put the chopped walnuts and dates in a basin and pour over the boiling water. Add the bicarbonate of soda. Rub together the margarine and flour. Add the sugar and beaten egg. Pour in the nuts, dates and water and mix thoroughly. The mixture will be very soft. Put into a lightly-greased 2-lb (1-kg) loaf tin and bake slowly in the oven for 1½ to 2 hours.

Banana Tea Loaf

From Janet Ashenden, Linton, Burton-on-Trent, Staffordshire

This recipe is one that I have had for some time but have made additions and omissions to suit the occasion (omit the nuts if it is to be served to small children). The recipe below is the full-blown affair – which I use for village fête teas.

For the best results you should use the blackest bananas that you can find. This loaf freezes really well, and certainly improves with keeping – if you can!

Makes 1×2-lb (1-kg) loaf

7 oz (200 g) self-raising flour
¼ teaspoon bicarbonate of soda
½ teaspoon salt
3 oz (75 g) butter
6 oz (175 g) sugar
2 eggs, beaten

1 lb (450 g) very ripe bananas, mashed
4 oz (100 g) walnuts, coarsely chopped
4 oz (100 g) sultanas
2 oz (50 g) glacé cherries

Pre-heat the oven to 350°F (180°C), gas mark 4.

Grease a 2-lb (1-kg) loaf tin. Sift the flour, bicarbonate of soda and salt. Cream the butter and sugar until pale and fluffy, then add the egg a little at a time, beating well after each addition. Add the mashed bananas and beat again. Stir in the flour, walnuts, sultanas and cherries. Spoon into the prepared tin and bake in the oven for 1¼ hours until well risen and just firm. Turn out and cool on a wire rack. Keep for at least 24 hours before serving either sliced and buttered, or spread with a lemon glacé icing (made from 3 oz (75 g) icing sugar mixed to a spreading consistency with a little lemon juice and water) and then decorate with walnut halves.

Yoghurt Cake

From Mrs Dorothy Aikens, Wooburn Green, Buckinghamshire

This is a very versatile recipe which you can top with a water icing; cut in half, adding jam and cream to make a sponge; or fill with fresh fruit or a pie filling and cream to make a gâteau, which may be decorated on the top.

Makes 1×9-in (23-cm) cake

1×5-oz (150-g) carton low fat natural yoghurt
¼ pint (150 ml) vegetable or corn oil

8 oz (225 g) cartons caster sugar
8 oz (225 g) cartons self-raising flour
2 teaspoons baking powder
2 eggs

Pre-heat the oven to 325°F (160°C), gas mark 3.

Grease and base line a 9-in (23-cm) round cake tin. Mix all the above ingredients together well and place in the prepared tin. Cook in the centre of a moderate oven for 1 to 1¼ hours, until firm to the touch. Leave in the tin to cool.

A quick and easy way to measure out this cake is to use the yoghurt carton as a measure. Mix 1 carton each of yoghurt and oil, 2 of sugar, 3 of flour plus the baking powder and eggs.

Viennese Fingers

From Mrs Frances Williams, Craig-y-don, Llandudno, Gwynedd

Much enjoyed by many church-goers at our Overseas Mission Meetings over the years!

Makes 12 fingers

4 oz (100 g) butter or margarine
1 oz (25 g) icing sugar
A few drops of vanilla essence
4 oz (100 g) plain flour

For the filling
  2 oz (50 g) icing sugar
  1 oz (25 g) margarine
  A few drops of vanilla essence
  ½ teaspoon boiling water

  4 oz (100 g) cooking chocolate, melted

Pre-heat the oven to 350°F (180°C), gas mark 4.
Cream the butter or margarine, icing sugar and vanilla essence together.
Add the flour gradually and mix well. Using a large nozzle and an icing bag,
pipe 2-in (5-cm) lengths on to greased baking trays. Bake in the oven for 20
minutes or until light golden brown. When cooled, mix the filling
ingredients together thoroughly. Sandwich the biscuits together in pairs
with the filling and dip the ends in melted chocolate.

Grannie's Lemon

From Mrs Rachel Mainwaring-Burton, Beaconsfield, Buckinghamshire

Known as 'Grannie's Lemon' among our children and grandchildren, I
collected this recipe from my mother's cookery book and she had it from
her mother's friend, so it's more correctly 'Great-Gran's Lemon'.

Makes 6 pints (3.4 litres)

12 lemons	*4 pints (2.25 l) boiling water*
6 lb (2.75 kg) preserving sugar or	*4 oz (100 g) tartaric acid powder*
* granulated cane sugar*	*(not cream of tartar)*

Peel the lemons very thinly, using a potato peeler to obtain the yellow zest
only, then squeeze out the juice. Put the peel in a large bowl, with the
lemon juice. Add the sugar and boiling water, and lastly the tartaric acid
powder. Stir until dissolved. Keep stirring until the mixture is cold. Then
scald or sterilise about 6 squash bottles or 7 wine-vinegar bottles. Strain out
the peel, and save with the lemon pips for use in marmalade-making, if
liked.
This traditional lemon juice keeps for several weeks.

❦ SUMMER SUNDAY LUNCHES ❦

Roy Castle's
Almond and Watercress Soup ○

It cuddles you on a cold day and, when chilled, refreshes you on a hot one. If the weather is changeable, keep dashing from oven to fridge!

Serves 2

1 bunch watercress	1 oz (25 g) butter
1 stick celery, finely chopped	1 oz (25 g) flour
½ pint (300 ml) milk	¾ pint (450 ml) vegetable stock
½ pint (300 ml) single cream	3 tablespoons ground almonds
Rind of 1 lemon	Salt and pepper

Clean the watercress and save a quarter of it for garnishing. Chop the rest very finely. Put the chopped watercress and celery in a saucepan with the milk, cream and the carefully peeled zest of a lemon and bring to the boil. In a larger saucepan, melt the butter, stir in the flour and cook them together for a few minutes without letting the flour brown. Blend in the vegetable stock, a little at a time, to make a thick smooth sauce. Stir in the milk and cream mixture, then the almonds and season to taste. Cook gently over a low heat for 10 minutes. Remove the lemon rind, leave the soup to cool a little and put it in the refrigerator to chill. When it is cold, check the seasoning again and garnish it with the remaining watercress.

Sir Brian Rix's Mango Fool ○

My favourite quick, delicious pudding!

Serves 4

2×14-oz (400-g) tins mangoes
½ pint (300 ml) double cream
Grated nutmeg

Strain then sieve the mangoes. Whip the cream and mix with the mangoes. Add a little of the juice if the fool is very thick. Sprinkle with the grated nutmeg and serve chilled, in individual glasses.

Grape Cream ○

From Mrs Helen Robertson, Radford Semele, Leamington Spa

Here is a very superior 'pud' for when the vicar comes to lunch – and it is easy for a Sunday because the preparation is done the day before! Very fattening!

Serves 4

1½ lb (750 g) white or black grapes
½ pint (300 ml) double cream
4 oz (100 g) soft light brown sugar

¼ pint (150 ml) thick natural yoghurt
4 oz (100 g) demerara sugar

The night before, de-pip the grapes, but do not peel (seedless grapes are good, only needing to be cut in half). Whip the cream until it is stiff. Fold the grapes into the cream. Put in a shallow ovenproof dish and cover with cling film. Leave in the refrigerator overnight.

The next day, before sitting down to the first course, put the grill on to maximum. Between courses, take the pudding from refrigerator, remove the cling film and spread the sugar in a thick layer over the top. Toast under the very hot grill for a few moments. Don't leave it for a second, or when you return there will be only a burnt offering! When the sugar begins to turn to toffee, remove at once and serve.

Serve the cream in small glass dishes.

Raspberry Brûlée ○

From Mrs Sue Harrison, Watton, Thetford, Norfolk

Serves 4

1 lb (450 g) fresh or frozen
 raspberries
¼ pint (150 ml) double cream

Pre-heat the grill. Place the raspberries to cover the bottom of a flameproof dish. Whip the double cream as thick as possible. Fold the yoghurt into the cream with a metal spoon. Cover the raspberries with the cream mixture. Completely cover all the cream mixture with demerara sugar, thickly spread. Place under the grill for approximately 1 minute until the sugar caramelises, but do not let the cream start to bubble through. Place in the refrigerator overnight or for at least 4 hours before serving.

Heavenly Banana Pie ○

From Anne and Tony Butterfield, Dale House Hotel, Kettlewell, North Yorkshire

Serves 4

3 medium-sized bananas
2 egg whites
8 oz (225 g) sugar
A pinch of salt

½ teaspoon lemon juice
8 oz (225 g) shortcrust pastry
Whipped cream to garnish
Chopped nuts

Pre-heat the oven to 325°F (160°C), gas mark 3.

Sieve the bananas, add the unbeaten egg whites, sugar, salt and lemon juice. Beat well until light and fluffy. Line an 8-in (20-cm) flan dish with the prepared pastry. Pour in the banana mixture. Bake for 20 to 30 minutes. Don't be tempted to cook the pie for longer!

When the pie is cold, serve it topped with whipped cream and sprinkled with nuts.

Lemon Giddy ○

From Ellsie Russell, Fleet, Hampshire

Ideal for summertime.

Serves 4

6 oz (175 g) caster sugar
4 oz (100 g) unsalted butter
Grated rind and juice of 2 large
 lemons

4 fresh eggs, separated
8 trifle sponges

Beat the sugar and butter until light and fluffy. Stir in the grated rind and juice of the lemons plus the egg yolks. Beat the egg whites until they form soft peaks, then fold into the mixture. Split the sponges and use them to line the bottom of a 2-pint (1.2-l) basin. Layer with some of the mixture, then more sponge. Follow this pattern until the basin is full, finishing with sponge. Cover with foil and weigh down with a saucer and some tins. Leave in the refrigerator for 24 hours before turning out of the basin to serve.

Serve smothered with cream!

Lemon Pudding ○

From Mrs B. Armstrong, Manchester

Serves 4

1½ oz (40 g) butter
6 oz (175 g) caster sugar
4 eggs, separated

1 pint (600 ml) milk
Grated rind and juice of 2 lemons
2 oz (50 g) plain flour, sifted

Pre-heat the oven to 400°F (200°C), gas mark 6.
Cream the butter and sugar together until light and fluffy. Mix the egg yolks
with the milk, lemon rind and juice. Beat into the butter and sugar mixture,
then add the flour, stirring well to avoid lumps. Whisk the egg whites until
stiff, then fold them into the other ingredients. Pour in a buttered 8-in
(20-cm) soufflé dish and place in a roasting tin of water. Bake for 30 minutes.
This pudding can be served hot, but is nicer cold.

Richard Briers'
Strawberry Ice-Cream

Home-made ice-cream is really yummy! It is expensive to make and very
fattening so you only make it on special occasions and serve it in small
portions. The name strawberry probably comes from the custom of placing
straw between the rows to protect the fruit.

Serves 4

8 oz (225 g) strawberries
3 eggs, separated

3 tablespoons icing sugar
½ pint (300 ml) thick cream

Wash and hull the strawberries, then mash them to a pulp. Whisk the egg
yolks and the sugar together to make a thick foam. Whip the cream until it
is stiff. Fold the cream and the mashed strawberries into the egg yolks.
Whisk the egg whites until they are stiff and fold them in. Pour into a mould
and freeze for about 5 hours.

Fast Fruit Pudding! ○

From Isabel Ewart, Production Assistant, Religious Broadcasting, Radio

Serves 4

½ pint (300 ml) Greek yoghurt or double cream (depending on your waistline)
1×11-oz (300-g) tin mandarin

oranges, drained
1×11-oz (300-g) tin pineapple, drained and crushed
A dash of cointreau

Mix together the yoghurt or cream and the fruit. Add cointreau to taste. Whip up the mixture with a whisk to mix the fruit and yoghurt thoroughly. Refrigerate for 30 minutes before serving.

For a more upmarket version of this recipe, use fresh pineapple. Slice the pineapples into 2 and scoop out the middle. Chop the pulp finely and return this with the rest of the mixture to the pineapple shells.

Summer Pudding ○

From Nigel Hepper, Bible plants expert from Kew Gardens

I like to make this pudding when the fruit is in season, then freeze it and eat it instead of a heavy plum pudding, after the turkey on Christmas Day (we have Christmas pudding another day). Raspberries are my favourite fruit. The recipe has been a favourite family recipe which I have known since I was a little boy, when my father grew a lot of soft fruit. The proportions of fruit can, of course, be altered, but it is essential to have raspberries as the main ingredient.

Serves 4 to 6

1 lb (450 g) raspberries
8 oz (225 g) redcurrants
4 oz (100 g) blackcurrants

5 oz (150 g) sugar
7–8 slices medium thick white bread, buttered

Cook the fruit with the sugar over a medium heat for 3 to 5 minutes until the sugar has melted and the juices run. Line a 1½-pint (900-ml) pudding basin with the bread, butter side out, pressing the slices well together and filling in any gaps with small pieces. Pour in the fruit and cover with another slice of bread. Place a small plate on top, to fit exactly inside the rim of the bowl, and place a 3-lb (1.5-kg) weight on that. Leave overnight in the refrigerator. Before serving, turn out on to a dish and, if liked, cover with custard, or serve really cold, with cream.

4
Autumn

❀ HARVEST FESTIVAL ❀

'While the earth remaineth, seedtime and harvest, and cold and heat, and summer and winter, and day and night, shall not cease.'
(Genesis 8 : 22)

The time of the Harvest Festival varies according to the location and weather, but it is usually September or early October. The Harvest thanksgiving service at church is a relatively recent idea, being introduced by the eccentric R. S. Hawker, Vicar of Morwenstow, Cornwall, in 1843.

Harvest thanksgiving is a time to give thanks to God for the harvest and it is always a popular church service. The congregation take fresh fruit, vegetables, bread and, today, canned foods, which are blessed and then distributed to the poor and elderly. Traditional hymns sung at this service are, 'We Plough the Fields and Scatter' and 'Come Ye Thankful People, Come'.

Church harvest suppers are still a feature of parish life, where the dessert is invariably an apple dish! The original harvest supper, however, would have been a huge feast provided by the farmer for all the workers who had reaped and collected the harvest. This was a time of great celebration, drinking, eating, and revelry, after the strenuous effort of the harvest. In Scotland, this meal was called 'Kim-Feast', in eastern England, 'Harkey', in the West Country, 'Harvest Frolic', and in northern England, 'Harvest Home' or 'Mell Supper', the word 'mell' coming from the Norse word meaning 'corn'. Labourers, called 'faggers', were usually hired specially for the task of reaping the harvest and a Harvest Lord would be appointed to oversee the workers. The reaping of the very last sheaf of corn was treated with great ceremony as it was believed to harbour the Corn Spirit. It was carefully cut and twisted into a corn dolly, which was carried home on top of the last load and given pride of place at the harvest supper.

Cliff Richard's Leek and Potato Soup ◯

Serves 4

2 oz (50 g) butter
1 lb (450 g) potatoes, peeled and cut
  into cubes
2 onions, roughly chopped
2 pints (1.2 l) chicken stock

1 teaspoon mixed herbs
8 oz (225 g) leeks, cut into 1-in
  (2.5-cm) pieces
¼ pint (150 ml) natural yoghurt

Melt the butter in a large saucepan and sauté the potatoes and onions for a few minutes. Add the stock, herbs and leeks. Simmer for about 10 minutes until the potatoes are cooked. Allow to cool for 10 minutes. Mix in the yoghurt, then put the soup through a blender at maximum speed. Re-heat gently before serving, but do not allow the soup to boil.
    Can be served hot or cold.

Dame Cicely Saunders' Harvest Mushrooms ◯

I am particularly fond of this because all Poles love mushrooms and go mushroom hunting in the autumn, and my husband, being Polish, greatly enjoys it.

Serves 4 to 5 as an hors d'oeuvre

1 lb (450 g) small button
  mushrooms
1 clove garlic
¼ teaspoon salt
3 fl oz (85 ml) oil

2 fl oz (50 ml) wine vinegar
Pepper to taste
1 small onion, very finely chopped
  or minced
1 tablespoon parsley, chopped

Wash, peel if necessary, and dry the mushrooms. If they are small, leave them whole, but if they are large, you may prefer to slice them. In a china or glass bowl crush the garlic clove with the salt. Slowly whisk in the oil, then the vinegar. Continue whisking until it turns a nice yellow colour. Then mix in the pepper, onion and parsley, and lastly the mushrooms. Stir the mushrooms around to coat them evenly. Leave them, covered, to marinate for at least 1 hour, longer for larger mushrooms, stirring occasionally.
    The mushrooms can be kept for several days if kept tightly covered in a refrigerator, so they can be prepared well in advance.

Harvest Home Casserole

From Mrs M. McDermott, Lisburn, Northern Ireland

Serves 4

2 oz (50 g) butter
1 onion, sliced
1 small green pepper, skinned, de-
* seeded and chopped*
1 small red pepper, skinned, de-
* seeded and chopped*

1 lb (450 g) vegetable marrow, cut
* into 1-in (2.5-cm) cubes*
4 oz (100 g) mushrooms (optional)
1 lb (450 g) pork pieces or pork fillet
1 tablespoon tomato purée
1 chicken stock cube, dissolved in
* ½ pint (300 ml) water*

Pre-heat the oven to 350°F (180°C), gas mark 4 if you are going to casserole the dish.

Melt the butter in a saucepan and fry the onion until clear and soft. Add the peppers, marrow pieces, and mushrooms, if using. Prepare the pork pieces by removing any fat and gristle and cutting into fork-sized pieces. Add these to the saucepan. Stir in the purée and stock. Cover with a lid and cook gently for 1 hour, or alternatively put in a casserole, cover and put in the oven for approximately 1 hour, or until the meat is tender.

Serve with boiled potatoes.

Claire Rayner's Aspic Tart ○

A fancy-looking but very simple dish!

Serves 4

1×8-in (20-cm) pre-baked pie shell
1 lb (450 g) lightly cooked
* vegetables (fried onions, glazed*
* baby carrots, beans, peas, chopped*
* celery, etc.)*

Well-flavoured aspic made with:
½ oz (15 g) gelatine
1 pint (600 ml) clear chicken stock
Sherry to taste

Arrange the cooked vegetables in attractive patterns in the pre-baked pie shell. Dissolve the gelatine in a little warmed stock, then mix into the stock, adding sherry to taste. Cover the tart with aspic and leave to set.

Jill Gascoine's Courgette and Cheese Soup

I just made it up and it's from a cookery book I'm writing. It's vegetarian and can be served as a main course with some salad and a nice piece of chunky wholemeal bread.

Serves 4

1½ pints (900 ml) vegetable stock (Vecon or stock cubes can be used if necessary)
1 large onion, chopped
4–5 courgettes (depends on how thick you want it), chopped
1 clove garlic, chopped (optional)
Salt and pepper

A pinch of mixed herbs (or to taste)
4 oz (100 g) Brie cheese, cut into cubes
2 oz (50 g) fresh Parmesan cheese, grated
Paprika and freshly chopped parsley to garnish

Place the stock, onion, courgettes and garlic in a large saucepan and season to taste with salt, pepper and mixed herbs. Bring to the boil and simmer for about 10 minutes until the vegetables are tender. Transfer to a food processor or blender and blend until smooth. Return to the saucepan, add the Brie cheese and simmer and stir until the cheese melts. Put into bowls and grate fresh Parmesan cheese on to the top. Sprinkle with paprika and freshly chopped parsley.

Stuffed Aubergines

From Samantha Paul, Secretary to Organiser, Religious Broadcasting, Radio

I like this attractive dish because it always makes me feel really healthy, with all the fresh vegetables and nuts. It has an interesting texture and impresses people who think you've gone to heaps of trouble when actually it's really easy!

Serves 2

1 large aubergine
Salt
1 onion, chopped
1 tablespoon sunflower or corn oil
1 clove garlic, chopped
2 small tomatoes, chopped
2 small courgettes, chopped

3 oz (75 g) mushrooms, chopped
1 oz (25 g) brown breadcrumbs (optional)
1 teaspoon mixed herbs
4 oz (100 g) cashew nuts, chopped
Salt and pepper
4 oz (100 g) Cheddar cheese, grated

Pre-heat the oven to 400°F (200°C), gas mark 6.

Cut the aubergine in half lengthways and sprinkle with salt. Leave to stand. Meanwhile, fry the onion in the oil until golden brown, then add the garlic, tomatoes, courgettes and, after a minute, the mushrooms. Rinse off the salt from the aubergine and gouge out the flesh, ensuring that sufficient flesh is left to form a shell. Add the flesh to the courgette mixture. If the mixture is very wet, add some breadcrumbs to stiffen it. Stir in the herbs and the chopped nuts and season to taste with salt and pepper. Remove from the heat. Press the mixture into the aubergine shells and top with the grated cheese. Bake in the oven for 20 minutes and if possible, grill for a couple of minutes until the tops are crispy and golden brown.

Serve on a bed of brown rice with soy sauce.

Red Cabbage and Apples ○

From Hazel Treadgold, Central President of The Mothers' Union 1983–1988

This is a very simple but quite delicious dish.

Serves 4

3 lb (1.5 kg) red cabbage, finely sliced
2 large Bramley apples, peeled and cored
2 medium-sized onions, sliced
1 teaspoon mixed spice
Peel of 1 orange

1 teaspoon white sugar
Salt and black pepper to taste
1 teaspoon chopped parsley
1 bay leaf
A pinch of thyme
2 tablespoons white wine vinegar
2 tablespoons red wine vinegar

Pre-heat the oven to 250°F (120°C), gas mark ½.

Place the sliced cabbage in a large saucepan with 1 in (2.5 cm) of boiling water and simmer for 3 to 4 minutes, then drain. Beginning with the cabbage, layer the cabbage, apples and onions in an ovenproof dish, ending with a layer of cabbage, and placing the spices, seasoning and herbs in the middle layer. Pour over the white and red wine vinegars, cover and bake in a low oven for 2 to 3 hours. Stir before serving and remove the orange peel.

Nerys Hughes' Pear Chutney

Makes about 4 lb (1.75 kg)

3 lb (1.5 kg) pears, peeled, cored and
sliced
1 lb (450 g) onions, skinned and
chopped
1 lb (450 g) green tomatoes, wiped
and sliced
8 oz (225 g) seedless raisins,
chopped

1½ lb (750 g) demerara sugar
¼ teaspoon cayenne pepper
¼ teaspoon ground ginger
2 teaspoons salt
5 peppercorns, in a muslin bag
1¾ pints (1 l) malt vinegar

Put all the fruit and vegetable ingredients into a pan, with no added liquid, and simmer gently until tender. Add the remaining ingredients and simmer until the chutney reaches a thick consistency, with no excess liquid. Remove the bag of peppercorns, pot in sterile jars and cover.

Fruit Chutney

From Mrs Edna A. M. Cattermole, New Longton, near Preston

Makes about 4 lb (1.75 kg)

3 lb (1.5 kg) apples, finely chopped
2 lb (1 kg) tomatoes, finely chopped
1 lb (450 g) seedless raisins, finely
chopped
1½ lb (750 g) onions, finely chopped

2 oz (50 g) mustard seed
1 teaspoon ground ginger
½ teaspoon cayenne pepper
1 pint (600 ml) vinegar

Place all the ingredients in a saucepan and boil for 45 minutes, stirring with a wooden spoon to stop the mixture sticking to the pan. Remove from the heat and pot in sterilised jars.

Marrow Lemon Curd

From Mrs Mary L. Lenihan, Bakewell, Derbyshire

Costwise, this is very economical and children love it.

Makes about 3 lb (1.5 kg)

2 lb (1 kg) marrow, seeded and
chopped
2 lb (1 kg) granulated sugar

Finely grated rind and juice of 3
lemons
4 oz (100 g) butter

Steam the marrow until tender, then pulp it. Place in a saucepan with sugar, lemon rind and juice. Stir over a gentle heat until the sugar has dissolved. Bring to the boil and simmer for about 25 to 30 minutes until thick and creamy. Bottle and cover.

To make *Marrow Curd Tarts*, beat 1 egg, stir in 4 tablespoons of milk, and mix into 8 oz (225 g) marrow lemon curd. Pour into a pastry case or small cases. Cook in the oven at 400°F (200°C), gas mark 6 for about 15 minutes until set.

Superior Apple Tart

From Mr Les Wiltsher, Shillington, Hitchin, Hertfordshire

I have been widowed for fifteen years, and in that time my skill as a cook has improved tremendously. When I have friends in they always sing the praises of my pastry, and my recipe for a rather superior apple tart.

Makes 1 × 10-in (25-cm) tart

12 oz (350 g) self-raising flour
A pinch of salt
3 oz (75 g) butter
3 oz (75 g) lard
2 large eggs, separated
*3 large cooking apples, peeled, cored
and quartered*

1 oz (25 g) butter
1 tablespoon honey
3 oz (75 g) sultanas or raisins
For the egg custard
A few drops of vanilla essence
½ pint (300 ml) milk

Pre-heat the oven to 400°F (200°C), gas mark 6.
Sieve half the flour into a bowl, add the salt, butter and lard, then cream them together with a strong knife. Add the remaining flour and rub in until you have a breadcrumb consistency. Form into pastry by adding the whites of the 2 eggs, again using the knife. Place the pastry in a plastic bag and put in the refrigerator for at least 4 hours. Simmer the apples until soft in a mixture of butter and honey. Wash the sultanas or raisins well in boiling water then add them to the mixture. Leave to cool. Roll out the pastry and line a 10-in (25-cm) flan ring. When rolling out the pastry you may find it helps to roughly form it by hand as this mixture makes a very short pastry. Fill it with the apple mixture and bake it in the oven for 20 minutes, then reduce the heat to 325°F (160°C), gas mark 3 and cook for a further 20 minutes.

To make the egg custard to serve with the tart, beat the egg yolks and add a few drops of vanilla essence. Boil just under ½ pint (300 ml) of milk and slowly add this to the egg yolks, stirring all the time. Return to the saucepan and re-heat, stirring all the time and making sure it doesn't boil.

Battered Apples

From Mrs T. M. Swales, Taunton, Somerset

Serves 4

2 eggs, beaten
2 oz (50 g) flour
1 oz (25 g) caster sugar
½ pint (300 ml) milk
A pinch of salt

4 cooking apples, peeled and cored
1 oz (25 g) butter
Sufficient brown sugar to fill the
  cavities

Pre-heat the oven to 325°F (160°C), gas mark 3.
  Make a batter by mixing the well-beaten eggs, flour, sugar, milk and salt.
Place the apples in a well-greased pie dish and put a knob of butter at the
bottom of each cavity. Fill each cavity with brown sugar and top with
another knob of butter. Pour the batter around the apples and bake in a
moderate oven for 45 minutes to 1 hour until golden brown.

Spicy Apple Cake

From Mrs Ruby M. E. Purdy, Belfast, Northern Ireland

This is a great favourite with my family.

Makes 1×8-in (20-cm) cake

3 oz (75 g) margarine
6 oz (175 g) self-raising flour
2 oz (50 g) sugar
1 large egg
3 fl oz (85 ml) (approx.) cold water
3–4 apples, peeled, cored and cut
  into thick wedges

For the topping
  3 oz (75 g) sugar
  2 teaspoons cinnamon
  Margarine

Pre-heat the oven to 350°F (180°C), gas mark 4.
  Rub the margarine into the flour until the mixture resembles fine
breadcrumbs. Add the sugar. Beat the egg and mix with the water. Stir into
the dry mixture to form a soft dough. Spread into a 7- or 8-in (18- or 20-cm)
sandwich tin. Press the apples into the dough. Mix the sugar and cinnamon
and sprinkle it over the dough, then dot the top with margarine. Bake in a
moderate oven for about 30 minutes until the apples are tender.
  The cake can be served with custard or cream, or eaten cold as cake.

David Alton's Apple Jam

This is a traditional Irish recipe, and is delicious on hot scones or pancakes.

Makes about 5 lb (2.25 kg)

5 lb (2.25 kg) apples   *4 pints (2.25 l) water*
12 whole cloves   *4 lb (1.75 kg) sugar*

Pre-heat the oven to 225°F (110°C), gas mark ¼.

Wash and quarter the apples. There is no need to peel or core them. Place them in an ovenproof dish and add the cloves and the water. Cover, with aluminium foil if necessary. Cook overnight at the bottom of the oven. Next day strain the apples through a jelly bag or a clean, white pillowcase; do not squeeze. Measure the liquid into a large saucepan and for every cupful add a cupful of sugar. Heat to dissolve the sugar and bring to the boil for about 10 minutes or until a little of the mixture gels on a cold saucer. Be careful here, as over-boiling will produce a syrup which will just get thicker without setting. Pour into jars which have been warmed in the oven and cover with waxed discs and lids.

The Archbishop of Canterbury's Mulberry and Apple Summer Pudding ○

This dessert is one of my favourite recipes because mulberries used to drop into our garden in St Albans from a neighbouring tree. They have become my favourite fruit.

Serves 4

2¼ lb (1 kg) mulberries   *¾ pint (450 ml) water*
2 cooking apples   *Stale white bread*
1 lb (450 g) sugar

Wash the mulberries. Peel, core and thinly slice the apples. Dissolve the sugar in the water and boil rapidly for 5 minutes. Add the fruit to the sugar solution and simmer for about 10 minutes until pulpy. Sieve through an aluminium sieve. Slice the bread thinly, cutting off the crusts. Use it to cover the bottom of a china soufflé dish. Then spoon in enough of the purée to cover the bread completely. Add another layer of bread, and continue with alternate layers of bread and fruit pulp until the dish is full. Place a small plate on the top, weighted down with a 1-lb (450-g) weight, and leave overnight before turning out the pudding.

Serve with whipped cream.

Chris Stuart's
Blackberry and Apple Meringue Pie

I was told about the dish by a member of the Women's Institute who I interviewed on the radio one morning. 'You will like this one,' she said. I went straight home, plundered the hedge for blackberries and set about the relatively straightforward task of preparing it. I won't say the first mouthful changed my life, but it reawakened an appetite for the sweet things of life I thought I had left behind with my childhood years. Have a bash yourself, along these lines . . .

Serves 4

8 oz (225 g) shortcrust pastry
1 lb (450 g) lightly stewed and
  sweetened blackberry and apple

2–3 egg whites
1 dessertspoon caster sugar

Pre-heat the oven to 350°F (180°C), gas mark 4.
  Roll out the pastry and use it to line an 8-in (20-cm) pie dish or flan ring. Fill with the fruit. Whisk the egg whites until stiff. Fold in the sugar, and spoon over the fruit and uncooked pastry, sealing the edges. Cook in a medium oven until the meringue is golden brown.
  'Then go jogging . . . preferably at regulo 6.'

Bramley Apple Lemonade ○

From Mrs Jennifer M. Merryweather, Southwell, Nottinghamshire

My husband's great-great-grandfather marketed the Bramley apple seedling here in Southwell. We still operate a garden centre here, and feel there is still nothing quite like the Bramley apple for cooking.

Makes about 8 pints (4.5 l)

2 lb (1 kg) Bramley apples
6 pints (3.4 l) cold water

1 lb (450 g) sugar
Rind and juice of 2 large lemons

Wash apples and cut into quarters. Core them, leaving skin on, and chop into small pieces. Put into bucket and cover with the cold water. Cover with cloth and stir night and morning for 1 week. Strain into another bucket. Add the sugar and the strips of lemon rind and juice. Stir until the sugar dissolves. Cover and leave for 24 hours. Strain into sterilised bottles (with screw tops). As this drink will be fizzy, leave to it settle for 2 to 3 weeks before drinking. It keeps well.

Edward Heath's Pumpkin Pie

I first enjoyed Pumpkin Pie when I travelled in the United States on a debating tour in the autumn of 1939. Now I delight in offering it to my American guests, much to their surprise, when they visit my home at Thanksgiving. This recipe I found on a visit to Athens, Georgia. It is one of some forty different recipes for this dish in my kitchen collection.

Serves 4

1 lb (450 g) pumpkin flesh with pith,
  skin and seeds removed
½ pint (300 ml) water
8 oz (225 g) shortcrust pastry
2 oz (50 g) apricot, plum or
  greengage jam

1 egg, beaten
1½ tablespoons brown sugar
1 teaspoon ground nutmeg
1 oz (25 g) currants, seedless raisins
  or sultanas

Pre-heat the oven to 400°F (200°C), gas mark 6.
  Cut the pumpkin flesh into 1-in (2.5-cm) cubes. Then place it in a large saucepan with the water, bring it to the boil and simmer, stirring occasionally to prevent sticking, for about 10 minutes. Drain and cool. Roll out the pastry and line an 8-in (20-cm) flan ring or pastry dish. Trim off the excess pastry from the edges of the flan and reserve the trimmings. Spread the pastry case with a thin layer of jam. Add the egg, sugar and most of the nutmeg to the cooled pumpkin flesh and either blend in a food processor, or mash with a fork until smooth. Mix in the dried fruit and pour the mixture into the pastry case. Sprinkle the remaining nutmeg on top of the pie and decorate with a lattice made from the pastry trimmings. Cook in the pre-heated oven for 15 minutes, then reduce the heat to 350°F (180°C), gas mark 4, and cook for a further 15 minutes or until the pastry is golden brown.
  Serve hot or cold. The pie is delicious when accompanied by thick cream.

Topping for Pumpkin Pie ○

From Sarah Cox, 1987 BBC Choirgirl of the Year

¼ pint (150 ml) double cream
Syrup from stem ginger to sweeten
¼ teaspoon ground ginger

2 oz (50 g) toasted walnuts, roughly
  chopped

Whip the cream, sweeten with the ginger syrup and add the ground ginger. Just before serving, cover the pumpkin pie with this cream and sprinkle with chopped, toasted walnuts.

✥ MICHAELMAS (29 SEPTEMBER) ✥

*'And there was war in heaven. Michael and his angels fought
against the dragon, and the dragon and his angels fought back. But
he was not strong enough, and they lost their place in heaven. The
great dragon was hurled down – that ancient serpent called the
Devil or Satan, who leads the whole world astray. He was hurled to
the earth, and his angels with him.'*
(Revelations 12 : 7 – 9)

Michaelmas is the feast day of St Michael and All Angels on 29
September.

St Michael was frequently depicted by Renaissance artists in
shining armour fighting the forces of evil. When Lucifer (the Devil)
revolted against God, it was Michael, the Archangel who defeated
him. In the book of Daniel (Daniel 10 : 13, 21; 12 : 1) he is portrayed
as protector of the people of Israel. He is also depicted as a winged
warrior, fighting the powers of darkness as he leads souls to Heaven,
away from Limbo and Hell. St Michael is the patron saint of horses,
soldiers and high places, like St Michael's Mount in Cornwall.

Michaelmas was traditionally a day for settling rent and bills. It
was also a time when farm labourers would seek new work at 'hiring
fairs'. Many of these fairs also sold geese, the most famous being
Nottingham's Goose Fair (which still takes place today although it
is now a fun fair and geese are no longer sold). Geese were nicely
fattened and at their best at this time of year, hence the custom of
eating goose at Michaelmas.

Michael's Michaelmas Macaroni

From Michael Wakelin, Producer, Good Morning Sunday

The link between this recipe and Michaelmas may at first seem rather remote. But when I point out that St Michael is the leader of God's army, an army marches on its stomach and this is a very filling meal; and add to that the fact that St Michael was seen in between the years 492 and 496 in the macaroni rich region of Monte de Gargano in Italy, it is clear to all why this is such an appropriate recipe for this time of year.

Serves 2

6 rashers streaky bacon, chopped
4 oz (100 g) mushrooms
Oil for frying
6 oz (175 g) macaroni
3 pints (1.75 l) water
Salt and pepper
1 oz (25 g) butter

1 oz (25 g) cornflour
½ teaspoon mustard powder
1 clove garlic, crushed (optional)
1 pint (600 ml) milk
6 oz (175 g) mature Cheddar cheese
2 small tomatoes, sliced

Grill the bacon until lightly crisped, and place on one side. Fry the mushrooms in a little oil until lightly golden, and place on one side. Boil the macaroni for about 10 minutes (check the packet) in the lightly salted boiling water. When soft, drain. To make the cheese sauce, melt the butter in a saucepan over a low heat. Stir in the cornflour, mustard powder and garlic until thoroughly mixed. Slowly add the milk, stirring continuously. Bring the thickening mixture to the boil and simmer gently for 2 minutes. Add two-thirds of the cheese and simmer for a further 2 minutes.

Mix the macaroni, bacon, mushrooms and cheese sauce, season to taste and place in a 2-pint (1.2-l) flameproof dish. Sprinkle the remaining cheese on top and arrange the sliced tomatoes on the cheese covering. Grill for 10 minutes and serve with a green vegetable.

❧ REMEMBRANCE SUNDAY ❧

Remembrance Sunday is on the Sunday nearest 11 November which is Armistice Day. It was at 11.00 a.m. on 11 November 1918 – 'the eleventh hour of the eleventh day of the eleventh month' – that an armistice brought the Great War of 1914–18 to an end, the war in which Britain alone lost nearly a million men in horrific battles, such as the Somme. Originally, there was a two-minute silence at the exact time the Armistice was signed.

Today, on the nearest Sunday to Armistice Day, we have a Remembrance service in churches throughout the land when we remember the dead of the two World Wars. The Royal Family watch a walk past of ex-Servicemen and women at Whitehall, London, and the Queen lays a wreath at the Cenotaph. There is a two-minute silence at 11.00 a.m. and poppies are sold in aid of the Royal British Legion.

Auntie Nellie's Ginger Cake

From Miss Muriel Kerr Wild, Ainsdale, Southport

This is not only a very good cake, but for me a symbol of a family friendship that goes back nearly a hundred years. The friend who gave it to me is 93 years old. One of her brothers was with the Liverpool Scottish Regiment in the First World War. She tells me that they made this cake and sent it out to him in France. A very sensible choice, because it travels and keeps well. The sad part of the story is that he was killed and did not come back.

Serves 12 to 18

4 oz (100 g) margarine or butter	*1½ teaspoons ground ginger*
4 oz (100 g) demerara sugar	*2 eggs, beaten*
2 tablespoons syrup	*8 oz (225 g) sultanas*
8 oz (225 g) plain flour	*2 oz (50 g) crystallised ginger,*
½ teaspoon bicarbonate of soda	*chopped*

Pre-heat the oven to 300°F (150°C), gas mark 2.

Grease and line a shallow 7- or 8-in (18- or 20-cm) square or rectangular baking tin with greaseproof paper. Grease the paper. Place the fat, sugar and syrup in a 5-pint (2.75-l) saucepan and melt them slowly. Add the sifted dry ingredients and the eggs and mix well. Then add the sultanas and chopped crystallised ginger. Pour into the lined tin and cook in a cool oven for 1½ hours. Do not be alarmed if the cake sinks a little in the middle. Leave to cool before removing from the tin.

❀ ST CATHERINE'S DAY (24 NOVEMBER) ❀

St Catherine of Alexandria, patron saint of lacemakers, wheel-wrights and scholars, was one of the most popular saints of the Middle Ages, but despite this relatively little is known about her. However, it is believed that she was martyred in AD 310. She was reputedly very beautiful, well read and a devout Christian. The Emperor Maxentius lusted after her, but she repelled his advances and it is said that she pleaded with him to stop the Christians being persecuted. In his anger he condemned her to death, by having her body broken on a spiked wheel. Miraculously during her torture the wheel broke, releasing her. Later she was beheaded and it is said she was then carried by angels to Mount Sinai where she was buried.

Cattern Cakes

From Mrs Janet Redmond, Yeovil, Somerset

St Catherine's feast day is still upheld in parts of Devon and Somerset. In Somerset, 24 November is known as 'Cattern's Eve' and the cattern cakes shaped like Catherine wheels are made from spiced pastry with currants in them. They are eaten hot with mulled ale, followed by cider.

Makes about 20 cakes

8 oz (225 g) plain flour
A pinch of mixed spice
1 teaspoon bicarbonate of soda
8 oz (225 g) sugar
2 heaped tablespoons ground almonds

8 oz (225 g) butter
2 heaped tablespoons currants or seedless raisins
1 egg, beaten

Pre-heat the oven to 400°F (200°C), gas mark 6.

Mix the flour, spice, bicarbonate of soda, sugar and ground almonds together. Melt the butter and stir it in, mixing to a stiff paste. Then add the currants or raisins and finally the beaten egg. Mix very thoroughly; the paste will be quite stiff. Turn out on to a floured board or table and roll out to ¼-in (3-mm) in thickness. Cut into ¼-in (3-mm) strips about 8 in (20 cm) long and roll round like a Catherine wheel, moistening with a little cold water to make the paste stick. Put on to a greased baking sheet and bake in a hot oven for 10 to 15 minutes. If preferred, the cakes can simply be cut out like small biscuits, but the wheel shape is traditional. They will keep for some time in an air-tight container.

✤ ST ANDREW'S DAY (30 NOVEMBER) ✤

St Andrew, a fisherman, was the first of the twelve Apostles to be chosen by Jesus and he is the patron saint of Scotland.

Jesus was referring to Andrew and his brother, Simon Peter, when he said he would make them *'fishers of men'* (Mark 1 : 16–18). One of Jesus's most famous miracles is known as the Feeding of the Five Thousand and it was Andrew who found the boy with five loaves of bread and two fish.

Andrew's life ended when he was crucified at Patras in Achaia. He was bound to the cross with rope and took two days to die. Since medieval times the X-shaped Saltire cross has therefore been the Scottish national symbol and adorns the Scottish flag (a white cross on a blue background).

There is no particular reason why St Andrew should be associated with Scotland except that it is believed that his relics were eventually brought to Fife, where a church was built to enshrine them and a city was named after him. At one time, St Andrew's Day would have been a great time of feasting, with haggis, malt whisky and sometimes cattern cake. However, nowadays this seems to be overshadowed by Burns' Night.

Sir Ranulph Fiennes'
Caledonian Cream Pudding ○

This is my favourite pudding recipe. To taste is to believe . . . it is paradise!

Serves 4 to 6

1 lb (450 g) curds of cottage cheese
2 tablespoons Dundee marmalade
2 tablespoons sugar
2 tablespoons brandy or malt
  whisky
1 tablespoon lemon juice

Mix all the ingredients together and beat with a whisk. Put in a dish and freeze before serving.

Athol Brose Pudding ○

From Margaret W. L. Johnson, Elstree, Hertfordshire

Serves 6

1 pint (600 ml) double cream
4 tablespoons thin, clear honey
1 large tot of whisky

Whisk all ingredients together until the mixture is thick and creamy.
Serve in 6 champagne glasses.

❀ AUTUMN SUNDAY LUNCHES ❀

Kaleidoscope Tart ○

From Miss Jane McAulay and Miss Mary Pirie, Drovers Rest Shoppe and
Tea Rooms, Llanwrtyd Wells, Powys, Wales

This tart is named after the Kaleidoscope organisation in Kingston-upon-
Thames, which is for drug addicts and other young people in need. The
group is so colourful and our recipe is a tribute to them. It has been made up
in our kitchen by us, and as far as we know is unique to us.

Serves 4

2 oz (50 g) lard
2 oz (50 g) margarine
8 oz (225 g) plain flour
1 oz (25 g) caster sugar
2 tablespoons water
1 egg yolk

For the filling
4 oz (100 g) caster sugar
4 oz (100 g) butter
2 eggs, beaten
4 oz (100 g) ground almonds
2 teaspoons ground ginger
Juice and grated rind of 1 lemon
2 oz (50 g) jam
1 large cooking apple, peeled, cored
  and thinly sliced
2 peaches, fresh or tinned, thinly
  sliced

Pre-heat the oven to 400°F (200°C), gas mark 6.

Put fat and flour into a bowl, and rub in the fat until the mixture resembles breadcrumbs. Add the sugar, water and egg yolk. Line an 8- or 9-in (20- or 23-cm) pie dish or tart tin, reserving a little pastry for decoration. Bake blind for about 20 minutes, then allow to cool. When cooled, put the pastry base on to a flat baking tray.

To make the filling, mix the sugar and butter together until creamy. Gradually add the eggs, then the ground almonds, ginger and 1 or 2 teaspoons of lemon juice. Paint the pastry base with jam and arrange the apple slices over the flan. Cover with a layer of peaches, then cover the fruit with the prepared mixture. Roll out the remainder of the pastry and decorate the top in a lattice pattern with strips of pastry. Bake in a low oven at 325°F (160°C), gas mark 3 for about 40 minutes until golden brown.

Serve hot or cold with cream or ice-cream. Just before serving, grate a little lemon peel over the top.

Osage Pie ○

From Mrs Eileen Turner, Wigan

This was sent to me by an old lady in America. It is called after the Osage Indians. We however call it 'Sunday Pudding' as it is so easy that the children used to make it before going to Sunday school. It will wait quite satisfactorily until popped in the oven when back from church, or the Salvation Army in our case. My father used to say, 'There is only one thing wrong with this pudding, there isn't enough of it.'

Serves 4

4 oz (100 g) granulated sugar	*1 raw cooking apple, chopped*
1 egg	*A few walnuts, chopped*
3 oz (75 g) self-raising flour	*1 teaspoon vanilla essence*
A pinch of salt	*A little milk to mix*
1½ teaspoons baking powder	

Pre-heat the oven to 350°F (180°C), gas mark 4.

Beat the sugar and egg with a wooden spoon. Sift the flour, salt and baking powder and stir into the mixture. Add the apple and nuts and lastly the vanilla essence and a little milk, so that the mixture is not too stiff, but not runny. Place in a greased 7-in (18-cm) pie dish and bake for about 40 minutes until the pie has risen and is lightly brown on top.

It is nice served with custard, or delicious with cream.

5
Jewish food

The major festivals in the Jewish Calendar are:

THE PASSOVER (PESACH)
which commemorates the rescue of the Jewish people
from slavery in Egypt.
THE FEAST OF WEEKS (SHAVUOT)
which commemorates the giving of the Ten Commandments to
Moses on Mount Sinai.
THE NEW YEAR (ROSH HASHANAH)
which commemorates the creation of the world.
THE DAY OF ATONEMENT (YOM KIPPUR)
which celebrates God's pardoning of the sins of the Jewish people.
TABERNACLES (SUCCOTH)
which serves as a reminder of the time when the Children of Israel
lived in temporary dwellings after the Exodus from Egypt.

Food plays a very important part in Jewish tradition as the observance of strict dietary laws is integral to Jewish home life. There are laws concerning the consumption of meat, fowl and fish; the mix of meat with milk; wine and grape juice products; and the food eaten at Passover. Food that is permissible is called 'Kosher', meaning 'acceptable', 'fit' or 'ritually usable'.

Topol's Aubergine Salad ○

This recipe is a favourite with Israelis, and is a particular favourite of the Topol family. It is very light in texture, and is suitable if there are vegetarians at the table. Because it is vegetable-based, it will go with almost any savoury dish, and is highly versatile.

This salad can be eaten as an hors d'oeuvre with bread, crackers, or pitta bread, or as a side salad to a main course.

2–3 aubergines, depending on size, trimmed
1 clove garlic (or to taste)
1–2 tablespoons mayonnaise or Tahina (if available)
Salt and pepper to taste
1 hard-boiled egg (optional)
Slices of red pepper to garnish

Pre-heat the oven to 325°F (160°C), gas mark 3.

Bake the aubergines in the oven for about 20 minutes until tender. Peel and strain off the juice. Put the aubergines, garlic, mayonnaise or Tahina and salt and pepper to taste in a blender or food processor and process until the ingredients are mixed together. If a thicker consistency is required, add the hard-boiled egg. Serve on a plate, decorated with slices of red pepper.

Joe Loss's Date and Nut Ring

I first had this when I went to tea at my daughter's and thought it so delicious that I asked her temporary housekeeper, Ann Bishop, if she would let my wife have the recipe!

Makes 1×9-in (23-cm) cake

6 oz (175 g) dates, chopped
6 oz (175 g) mixed nuts, chopped
4 oz (100 g) brown sugar
1 tablespoon flour
1 teaspoon baking powder
2 eggs, beaten
1 teaspoon vanilla essence
2 egg whites, whisked until stiff
A pinch of salt
2 tablespoons brandy or rum
Double cream to garnish

Pre-heat the oven to 350°F (180°C), gas mark 4.

Mix the dates, nuts and sugar thoroughly, and then add the flour, baking powder, eggs and vanilla essence. Fold in the egg whites and the salt. Put into a greased 9-in (23-cm) ring mould. Bake in a moderate oven for 30 minutes. When it is still warm, pour over the liquor. Turn out when cold, and decorate with whipped cream, nuts or fruit.

✿ THE SABBATH (SHABBAT) ✿

According to Jewish Law, the Sabbath (Saturday) is the seventh day of the week. It begins before sundown on Friday and ends at sundown on Saturday night when three stars are seen in the sky. This custom derives from the Torah which states that God created the world in six days and rested on the seventh, thereby setting an example to Jews to rest on this day. The Sabbath is a joyful time of spiritual refreshment and very much a day for the family. Contemporary Sabbath practices actually evolved as late as the sixteenth century. Prayers at the synagogue are important, but the Sabbath is celebrated in the home. It is inaugurated by the woman of the house, who traditionally lights two candles, before sundown, which burn for the duration of the Friday night meal. Then the man of the household will recite 'Kiddush', that is to say a blessing over the wine. This is followed by the blessing of the Sabbath bread or Cholla which is a plaited loaf baked specially for this meal. The grace or 'birkat hamazon' is said at the end of the meal.

The two rules of the Sabbath are 'Remember the Sabbath day to keep it holy' (the fourth of the Ten Commandments) and 'Do no manner of work'. The many categories of forbidden work include cooking, so the food for Friday night and Saturday has to be prepared in advance or left simmering over a slow flame that is lit before the Sabbath begins. This gave rise to a number of Sabbath dishes, such as the famous Cholent. This is a meat stew, including beans and potatoes, which is eaten by Jews the world over. It was created so that hot food could be eaten on the Sabbath without breaking Sabbath laws.

There are three Sabbath meals but it is the Jewish Friday night meal that is the equivalent of the Christian Sunday lunch, in that it is the main meal of the week, when the family gets together, wearing their best outfits and using the best crockery. It is customary for celebrants of the Sabbath to set the table before sundown on Friday, with a white table cloth kept specially for use on the Sabbath.

Traditionally prayers are said by the head of the household and special songs called 'zemirot' are sung. The end of the Sabbath is marked by the ceremony of 'havdalah', which symbolises the end of the 'separation' of the Sabbath from the rest of the week.

Rabbi Hugo Gryn's Cholent ○

I believe that the most important Jewish festival is actually the weekly Sabbath. A traditional dish and great favourite is the Cholent. To enable a Jewish family to enjoy a hot dish, especially in the winter months, without having actually to cook on the Sabbath, this dish is perfect. In my home-town the ovens of local bakers were used – who for a penny accepted the ready-prepared pots, put them into their ovens Friday afternoon and they were ready for collection after the morning service on Saturday. Nowadays people use their own kitchen ovens.

Serves 8 to 10

1 lb (450 g) red kidney beans (or a mixture of beans)
2 oz (50 g) medium pearl barley, washed
2 cloves garlic, chopped
1 medium onion, chopped
1 oz (25 g) plain flour (slaked in cold water)

1 oz (25 g) shmaltz (chicken fat) or its vegetarian equivalent
2 teaspoons salt
2 teaspoons paprika
A little fresh black pepper
6–8 oz (175–225 g) soup meat on the bone (flanken) (for non-vegetarians)

If using a mixture of beans, wash and soak these overnight on Thursday. It is advisable to throw off the first 2 or 3 soaks. On Friday morning discard the beans that are floating on the surface, rinse the beans again and cover generously with cold water. Mix together all the ingredients and bring to the boil early to mid-afternoon on Friday. Boil steadily for at least 10 minutes to destroy any toxins in the beans. Place in a cool oven at 275°F (140°C), gas mark 1 to continue cooking until lunchtime on Saturday (until you become an expert, inspect the pot from time to time to make sure that it doesn't dry out).

As an optional extra, you can add 6 to 8 eggs in their shell which will hard-boil in the mixture (do not be put off by the discolouring of the egg whites). Remove the eggs the next day and serve them as an hors d'oeuvre or chop them up with raw or slightly braised onion and season to taste. Alternatively, you may chop up the eggs with a mixture of onion and braised chicken livers.

Allow a leisurely rest of 2 or 3 hours after lunch for a Sabbath siesta.

Julia's Cholla Recipe ○

From Mrs Julia Abrahams, Clayhall, Ilford, Essex

This is a favourite and is used each Friday night in Jewish homes worldwide where candles are lit. Two are used, commemorating Friday, when two Manna fell from Heaven. Each day following, one fell. If one prefers a sweet version, just add more sugar.

Makes 2 loaves

1½ lb (750 g) strong white flour
2 teaspoons sugar or 1 teaspoon
icing sugar+1 teaspoon granulated
sugar
1 packet dried powdered yeast
(Allinsons, or Harvest Gold)

1 tablespoon oil
1 egg, beaten
½ pint (300 ml) warm water
2 teaspoons salt

Sieve the flour into a large bowl, add both sugars, yeast and oil. Mix well by hand or machine. Add the beaten egg, leaving some to brush on before baking. Slowly add some water – you may not need it all – and a little salt. Knead for 10 minutes by hand or 4 minutes in a mixer. When the dough is pressed with a finger and it springs back it is live and ready to shape.

To make plaited loaves, cut the dough into 6 equal-sized pieces. Roll each piece to a 9-in (23-cm) sausage shape. Join 3 pieces together at one end and loosely plait the dough, squeezing the pieces together at the other end. To make coiled loaves, cut the dough into 2 pieces and roll out into sausage shapes. Curl the dough into a spiral, tucking the end underneath. For dinner rolls, divide the dough into about 10 equal-sized pieces. Roll them into sausage shapes and curl them up into spirals, bringing the end up through the centre.

When shaped, place the dough on oiled baking trays and cover with large high plastic bag to allow space for them to rise. Tuck in the ends to keep the dough warm. Leave for 1½ to 2 hours in a warm place. Pre-heat the oven to 425°F (220°C), gas mark 7. When ready to bake, brush the loaves with egg, and sprinkle on mon (poppy seed) or sesame seed. Bake for 15 to 20 minutes in the centre of the oven for small rolls, or 30 minutes for larger ones. If the bottom sounds hollow when tapped they are well baked.

Rabbi Lionel Blue's
Egg, Onion and Parsley Pâté ○

This recipe uses only simple ingredients, but the end result has a lovely taste – especially if you let the flavours develop in the fridge. Eat with a white country loaf, toast or, best of all, Jewish plaited egg bread called Cholla. It was our family treat after three stars appeared in the sky on Friday evenings, and the Sabbath began.

The quantities here provide starters for 4 greedy diners or 6 calorie-conscious ones

2 large onions, chopped
2 oz (50 g) butter or margarine
4 tablespoons sunflower oil
1 teaspoon sugar

10 hard-boiled eggs, shelled and
  chopped
4 tablespoons parsley, chopped
Salt and freshly ground pepper

Fry 1 chopped onion in the butter or margarine and oil. Sprinkle with the sugar as the onion fries, so that it caramelises and turns a rich brown. Turn off the heat. Stir into the pan the chopped egg, the other finely chopped raw onion, the parsley, and plenty of salt and pepper. Bind them all together with the fat. Pack the mixture into pots or ramekins and chill for several hours. The pâté will firm up, the 2 types of onion combining flavours nicely.

Esther Rantzen's Grandmother's
Recipe for Chopped Liver ○

This is a traditional Jewish dish served mainly for the Sabbath evening meal.

Serves 4

1 large Spanish onion, sliced
Oil for frying
2 lb (1 kg) chicken liver (or calves'
  liver)

3–4 hard-boiled eggs
1 tablespoon melted chicken fat
  (optional)
Salt and pepper

Fry the sliced onion in a little oil for about 10 minutes until golden. Remove from the pan. Chop in a food processor for about 1 minute until very finely chopped. Place in a bowl. Fry the livers for about 10 minutes until well done. Chop in a food processor until smooth. Add to the onions. Reserve 1 egg yolk for garnish. Finely chop the remaining hard-boiled eggs in a food processor. Add to the liver and onions and mix to a smooth pâté. If it is not moist enough, a little of the pan juices may be added or about 1 tablespoon of chicken fat. Season to taste and garnish with chopped egg yolk.

CHANUKAH

This 'Feast of Lights' is a minor Jewish holiday observed for eight days in December, round about the same time as Christmas. The word 'chanukah' means 'dedication' in the sense of dedicating a place of worship and in this case it refers to the rededication of the Temple in Jerusalem by the Maccabees in circa 165 BCE. Chanukah marks the rescue of the Jewish faith and way of life from obliteration. The story goes that the Temple, considered sacred by all Jews, had been defiled by the Syrians in an attempt to stamp out the Jewish faith. However, they were driven out of the Temple by the army of Israel led by Judah Maccabee. According to the Talmud, these Jews then re-entered the Temple and prepared it for worship, but found just one lamp with only enough consecrated oil to burn for one day. To prepare more would have taken a week, but they could not wait that long, so they lit the lamp and miraculously it burned for eight days, allowing enough time for more oil to be prepared.

Traditionally, Chanukah is commemorated by the ritual lighting of the 'menorah', an eight-branched candelabra. The candles are lit for eight successive evenings – one candle more should be lit each day until all eight are burning, after which a hymn, Maoz Tzur, is sung. The menorah should be displayed in a window or doorway so that passers-by may be made aware of the 'miracle' of Chanukah.

Traditional celebrations include games, parties and the giving of gifts to children. In recent years the general festivities have become more elaborate. Homes are decorated and living room games are popular. On each night of this festival it is customary to give the children 'Chanuka gelt', Yiddish for Chanukah money, or other presents.

There are no prescribed foods for this Feast of Lights, but it is traditional to eat cheese pancakes, Latkes and doughnuts.

Rabbi Hugo Gryn's Latkes

This is very traditional and very basic. It is meant for 20 people. You can of course double the quantities.

Serves 20

8 lb (3.6 kg) potatoes, peeled and grated
2 large onions, grated
Salt and pepper
4 oz (100 g) medium matzo meal (packets of this can be bought in shops – it is like breadcrumbs which have been made out of unleavened bread)

2 tablespoons chicken fat, or machzik (a kosher vegetarian 'chicken fat') or oil
Oil for frying

Mix together the grated potato and onion. Drain off some of the liquid and add salt and pepper to taste. Stir in the medium matzo meal and chicken fat or machzik, or oil. Heat some oil in a frying pan, and when a piece of onion sizzles in it, drop in some tablespoons of the mixture. When they are brown, turn them over to brown on the other side. Drain them on a grid, and eat them hot. (They probably won't ever reach the grid.)

When the potatoes are grated they turn brown. Don't be put off by the colour, it doesn't affect the flavour or the appearance of the pancakes after they are fried.

If you have enjoyed the latkes as a savoury, you can go on to eat them as a sweet. Many Jews do. (You get marks for perseverance.) You can then reduce the quantity of onion in the latke mix; I personally don't. Eat them, then:
– with sugar
– with sugar and cinnamon
– with apricot jam
– with a little olive oil (to remember the Temple lamps rekindled by the Maccabees).

Serve the latkes with large glasses of hot lemon tea with a tablespoon of rum in each. This is a special festival tea called in Yiddish 'a literarish glez'l tay' (a literary little glass of tea).

These can be eaten with slivers of sweet and sour cucumber (classical and Russian), coleslaw, apple sauce, or spring onions.

❧ PASSOVER (PESACH) ❧

Passover is an eight-day festival commemorating one of the most important events in Jewish history, that is the rescue of the Jewish people from slavery in Egypt, and it is one of the five most important Holy days in the Jewish calendar.

There are strict guidelines regarding behaviour during Passover and these are found in Exodus, Chapter 12. It says that the Passover must be celebrated on 'the fourteenth of Nisan' (during the first month of spring) with a feast that does not contain leaven. The three main rules of Passover are:

– during the eight-day period no leaven or fermented grain is to be eaten or drunk. So this means that foods like cereals, spaghetti, malt vinegar, beer, ketchup, bread, cakes and pastries are all forbidden.

– Matza (unleavened bread) must be eaten. Other permitted foods include fresh vegetables, fresh fruit, dairy products, fish, soda water, brandy and meats.

– the Seder must be celebrated at home. This is a ritual meal where the Passover story from Exodus is recited for the benefit of the children. This is the highlight of Passover for which an elaborate meal is cooked and to which guests are often invited as it is traditionally a time when blessings should be shared with others, in particular with the less fortunate.

The story of Exodus is told by the father of the family who illustrates it by using various items of food, for example, an egg, the symbol of life, is dipped in salt water and bitter herbs are eaten, in sympathy with the 'bitter lot' experienced by their Jewish ancestors. A mix of nuts and apples represents the mortar used by Hebrew slaves in building cities for their masters. During the course of this story the youngest child in the family will traditionally ask the father four questions about the Passover. This is a joyful festival so the family table is decorated with the best china, candles, flowers and fruit. Each celebrant at the meal has a cup full of wine from which they take four sips as a symbol of joy.

Helen Shapiro's Passover Cinnamon Balls

These little darlings are a great favourite with most people at this festive season and I particularly like them because I love cinnamon. Passover is the celebration and memorial of when our people Israel were delivered from bondage in the land of Egypt. It is commanded by God in the Bible (Exodus, Chapter 23, verse 15, and Leviticus, Chapter 23, verses 4–8, etc.). As a Messianic Jew, it is also a time to reflect on my deliverance from bondage to sin, through the Messiah Yeshua who, as the Lamb of God, is fulfilment of the Passover message.

Makes approximately 40

3 egg whites
5 oz (150 g) caster sugar
2 teaspoons cinnamon
8 oz (225 g) ground almonds

2 teaspoons desiccated (not
  desecrated!) coconut (optional)
Icing sugar

Pre-heat the oven to 350°F (180°C), gas mark 4.
Beat the egg whites to a stiff froth. Add the sugar, cinnamon, ground almonds and coconut, if used, and mix thoroughly. Roll into small balls and place on a greased baking sheet. Bake in a moderate oven for 20 to 25 minutes until set. Put some icing sugar in a polythene bag and while the cinnamon balls are still warm shake them in the bag, one at a time, to coat them.
The addition of the coconut to the recipe keeps the cinnamon balls soft. Enjoy them!

Snowcake

From Mrs Julia Abrahams, Clayhall, Ilford, Essex

This cake contains no flour nor yeast, remembering when the Jewish people were sent out of Egypt to the desert for forty years. This fact is prominent in our Passover baking, still upheld in very many homes.

Makes 1×9-in (23-cm) cake

6 large eggs, separated
12 oz (350 g) caster sugar
2 tablespoons oil
8 oz (225 g) potato flour

Grated rind and juice of ½ lemon
2 tablespoons baking powder
Icing sugar
Jam (if you want a sandwich cake)

Pre-heat the oven to 375°F (190°C), gas mark 5.

Beat the egg yolks with the sugar and add the oil. Beat the egg whites to snow and add to the yolks. Add the potato flour, lemon rind and juice, and baking powder. Only mix in the ingredients with a metal spoon, and do not beat. Place the mixture in a greased 9-in (23-cm) round or square cake tin and bake in a moderately hot oven for 1 hour. When cool, sprinkle with icing sugar. If you want a sandwich cake, cut the cake in half horizontally, spread the centre with jam and sandwich the two halves together.

Luxury Matza Pudding ○

From Hilda Milestone, Edgware, London

This is made for the Jewish Passover festival. This was put into our synagogue magazine but I feel that it deserves wider publicity as everyone who has it goes crazy over it and says it is something like a Christmas pudding. Bread can be substituted for matzas. Best served hot.

12 oz (350 g) dried fruit (kosher raisins are obtainable and sultanas, if available)
1 apple, shredded
Pesach wine (sweet red), i.e. Palwins No 4 or 10
4 matzot

4 eggs, beaten
4 oz (100 g) margarine, cut into pieces
6 oz (175 g) brown sugar
2 level tablespoons matzo meal
Mixed spice and cinnamon to taste

Marinate the fruit in the wine for at least 30 minutes, but the longer the better, overnight if possible. Pre-heat the oven to 300°F (150°C), gas mark 2. Pour hot water over the matzot and soak until soft (boiling water softens the matzot quicker than cold and makes them less soggy). Drain the matzot and mash well, making sure no water is left. Add the beaten eggs, margarine and the other ingredients. Then add the fruit and some of the wine that it has been marinating in. Mix well and turn into a greased covered casserole dish (make sure the casserole is covered to get a good pudding effect). Bake in a cool oven for 1 to 1½ hours until browned through.

A Recipe For Life

From Mrs Vera Hirst, Local WRVS organiser, Littleborough,
Metropolitan Rochdale

This recipe was concocted by the late Marchioness of Reading (1894–1971), who was appointed the first-ever Chairman of the Women's Royal Voluntary Service. It is a jolly good recipe, the size of the slice doesn't matter, it's the mixture of the ingredients that's important.

> *Take equal parts of faith and*
>   *courage,*
> *Mix well with a sense of humour,*
> *Sprinkle with a few tears*
> *And add a large helping of kindness*
>   *to others.*
> *Bake in a good-natured oven and*
>   *dust with laughter.*
> *Remove all pity for self,*
> *Scrape away any self-indulgence*
>   *that is apparent,*
> *And serve in generous helpings.*

❧ BIBLIOGRAPHY ❧

ASHERI, M., *Living Jewish*
(Jewish Chronicle Pubs., 1980).

JONES, J. and DEER, B., *Cattern Cakes and Lace: a Calendar of Feasts*
(Dorling-Kindersley, 1987).

KERTZER, M. N., *What is a Jew?*
(Collier Macmillan, 1978).

KIGHTLY, C., *The Customs and Ceremonies of Britain*
(Thames & Hudson, 1986).

METFORD, J. C. J., *Dictionary of Christian Lore and Legend*
(Thames & Hudson, new edn., 1986).

SHUEL, B., *The National Trust Guide to the Traditional Customs of Britain*
(Webb & Bower, 1985).

UNTERMAN, A., *Jews: Their Religious Beliefs and Practices*
(Routledge, 1981).

WHITLOCK, R., *A Calendar of Country Customs*
(Batsford, 1978).

❧ INDEX ❧